MW01616611

15ᵀᴴ EDITION

Melaleuca
Quick Reference

Recommended uses for Melaleuca products
based on research and the clinical experiences
of health care professionals and veterinarians
and
Proven household solutions recommended by
people who use Melaleuca products every day

A handy companion to our more complete
The Melaleuca Wellness Guide book

For more Melaleuca information,
visit our web site, **www.rmbarry.com**

DISCLAIMERS:

RM Barry Publications is an independent publishing company and is not affiliated with or related to Melaleuca, Inc. We specialize in providing educational information to Melaleuca Marketing Executives about and related to Melaleuca, Inc. and its products. However the claims and information contained in the publications distributed or authored by RM Barry Publications are not endorsed, approved or sponsored by Melaleuca, Inc.

Every effort has been made to ensure that the information contained in this book is complete and accurate. However, neither the publisher nor the author is engaged in rendering professional advice or services to the individual reader. The ideas, procedures and suggestions contained in this book are not intended as a substitute for consulting with your physician. All matters regarding health require medical supervision. Each person's health needs are unique. To obtain recommendations appropriate to your particular situation, please consult a qualified health care provider. RM Barry Publications, its authors, and Melaleuca, Inc. shall have neither liability nor responsibility to any person or entity with respect to any loss, damage, or injury caused or alleged to be caused by any information or suggestion in this book.

This book is intended to supply educational information to users of products manufactured by Melaleuca, Inc. It should not be used as sales literature or for business promotion.

All product names in this book (in **_bold italics_**) are registered trademarks of Melaleuca, Inc. of Idaho Falls, Idaho.

Portions of this book were compiled or written by D.S. Church, Ph.D.

Published by:
RM BARRY PUBLICATIONS
P.O. BOX 3528
LITTLETON, CO 80161-3528

Toll-Free **1 (888) 209-0510**
Local (303) 326-0626
Fax (303) 568-0224

Web Site: **WWW.RMBARRY.COM**
E-mail: **INFO@RMBARRY.COM**

ISBN 978-0-9801117-8-1
Printed in the United States of America

For even more Melaleuca information ...

We sincerely hope you find this *Melaleuca Quick Reference* helpful. For more complete information, please order our 320 page book entitled *The Melaleuca Wellness Guide* which goes into greater depth on many of the conditions covered in this booklet. In addition, *The Melaleuca Wellness Guide* contains nearly ten times the information found in this booklet. Here's a brief description of its contents:

- An inspiring chapter on Melaleuca's company history and its founder.

- A chapter on *Melaleuca alternifolia* oil, its history, uses, and a comprehensive list of available research.

- A chapter on the health effects of toxic chemicals in household products.

- Chapters on grape seed extract, heart health, digestive health, depression, prostate health, eye health, glucosamine, head lice, menopause, boosting the immune system, and urinary tract infections.

- Over 200 health conditions with remedies and prevention strategies based on research and the clinical experiences of health care professionals.

- Over 150 home care problems with solutions recommended by people who use Melaleuca products every day.

- Over 215 ailments common to dogs, cats, horses, and farm animals with remedies recommended by experienced veterinarians, farmers, ranchers, and horse and pet lovers.

- A chapter on gardening and other alternative uses for Melaleuca products.

- A Melaleuca price comparison chart.

- A useful "Products Index" that references the various applications for each Melaleuca product, as well as a "Problems Index" to help you discover which products will help with your particular problem or condition.

- Plus there's much, much more!

Try a copy of

The Melaleuca Wellness Guide
Only US $12.50
Order your copy today! Call 1 (888) 209-0510

Table of Contents

Products Index

Use this index when you have a product and you want to discover what applications you can use it for. Use the Table of Contents on page 4 when you have a problem or condition and you want to discover which products will help. **Note:** This index covers the "Healthy Body" and "Healthy Home" chapters only.

The History of Tea Tree Oil

(Melaleuca alternifolia oil)

THE FIRST DISCOVERY OF TEA TREE OIL

For thousands of years, Bundjalung aborigines, a nomadic tribe that roamed eastern Australia, used the leaves of the Melaleuca alternifolia tree to treat various conditions. However, it wasn't until the late 1700s that the first Europeans learned of its healing powers.

In 1770, Captain James Cook (then a lieutenant in the British Royal Navy) landed the *H.M.S. Endeavor* at Botany Bay, near the site that would eventually become the city of Sydney. From there, he ventured into the snake-infested swampland of New South Wales. He discovered within this forbidding swamp groves of trees whose flowering blossoms were dripping with sticky, aromatic oil. The area had been named "Bungawalbyn," or "healing ground," by the aborigines.

Captain Cook observed the local aborigines applying crushed leaves from the trees directly to open wounds. In addition, the natives used the oil as an insect repellent and in healing mud packs. The aborigines also brewed a tea from its leaves. Tasting the tea, he found it to be spicy and invigorating. It was Captain Cook who gave the Melaleuca alternifolia tree its common name – the tea tree.

Sir Joseph Banks, a botanist accompanying Cook on his expedition, collected samples of the tea tree leaves and brought them back to England for further study. Captain Cook, impressed with the quality of the tea, gathered a generous supply of the Melaleuca leaves in order to brew tea for himself and his crew for their journey home. It is reported the tea helped prevent scurvy on the long voyage.

Although Sir Joseph Banks went on to serve as president of Britain's Royal Society for 40 years, nothing developed from his investigations of the Melaleuca leaves. The amazing healing properties of tea tree oil, for the most part, remained undiscovered by people outside of Australia. Meanwhile, European settlers who arrived in Australia near the end of the 18th century absorbed some of the well-known practices of the aborigines, including using local flora for medicinal purposes. Melaleuca alternifolia was widely used by the settlers as an effective treatment in the prevention of infection and even recognized for its properties by Denis Considen, the first assistant surgeon to the Colony. However, due to a lack of training and proper laboratory equipment, the true potential of the oil lay dormant for the next 150 years.

THE SECOND "DISCOVERY" OF TEA TREE OIL

Finally, in 1923, Dr. A. R. Penfold, an Australian government chemist working at the Technological Museum in Sydney, conducted the first in-depth investigation into tea tree oil. His studies focused on the properties of Melaleuca oil and the different compounds it contained. What he discovered was truly amazing. Through distillation, he was able to isolate the essential oil of the Melaleuca alternifolia tree. He found that the oil exhibited antiseptic and bactericidal properties 13 times stronger than carbolic acid. At the time, carbolic acid was the accepted, universal standard for treatment of infections. In 1925, he presented his findings to the Royal Society of New South Wales and England:

> *Melaleuca alternifolia is quite common, and exists in very large areas in the North Coast district of New South Wales. It yields 1.8% of an oil of pale lemon tint and is particularly recommended as a nonpoisonous, non-irritant antiseptic and disinfectant of unusual strength. The oil contains 50 to 60% of Terpenes (pinene, terpinene and cymene), from 6 to 8% of Cineole (accounting for the camphoraceous odor) and an alcohol terpineol, which supplies the pleasant nutmeg-like odor. The valuable antiseptic properties of the oil and its spicy flavoring should prove useful in dentrifices and mouthwashes.*

Penfold's scientific discoveries, accompanied by his personal enthusiasm, helped launch further studies into the power of tea tree oil. Australian doctors began experimenting with tea tree oil, using it to treat a variety of wounds and oral infections with great success. One of the first major references to tea tree oil appeared in *The Medical Journal of Australia* in 1930. Dr. E. M. Humphrey reported his findings with these words:

> *Dirty wounds, such as are frequently seen as the result of street accidents may be washed or syringed out with a 10% (tea tree oil) watery lotion, the solvent properties will loosen and bring away the dirt which is usually ground in, and the tissues will remain fresh and retain their natural color. The results obtained in a variety of conditions when it was first tried were most encouraging, a striking feature being that it dissolved pus and left the surfaces of infected wounds clean so that its germicidal action became more effective and without any damage to the tissues.*

This was something new, as most efficient germicides destroy tissue as well as bacteria. In addition, Dr. Humphrey found tea tree oil effective in abating sore throats and other naso-pharynx infections.

The same year, an article appeared in *The Australian Journal of Dentistry* reporting that tea tree oil is

> *"an antiseptic which more nearly answers the ideal than any I have previously tested in our special work; and in general surgery it should be of even greater value."*

Tea tree oil quickly became the antiseptic of choice among dentists because it was highly effective and did not damage healthy gum tissue.

The fact that tea tree oil had the ability to destroy pus and harmful bacteria, while at the same time leaving healthy tissue undamaged, helped propel it to prominence. No other antiseptic or germicide available at the time had that ability. The popularity of Melaleuca alternifolia oil grew and soon United States and British medical journals were reporting on tea tree oil's effectiveness. Diabetic gangrene, gynecological disorders, and fungal infections were all being effectively treated with Melaleuca oil.

When World War II broke out, both the Australian army and navy turned to tea tree oil and made it a vital part of every soldier's first aid kit. Infections in a war zone would soon lead to extended hospital stays and amputations. Quickly and effectively cleaning and disinfecting wounds was crucial to survival, and nothing worked like oil of Melaleuca. Australian soldiers stationed in tropical zones actively treated fungal foot infections as well as wounds with the oil.

At home, workers would often have their hands cut and scraped by metal shavings and filings while manufacturing shell casings and other metal implements important to the war effort. When tea tree oil was blended with machine cutting oil, these cuts and abrasions healed more quickly, and rarely became infected. So important to the war effort was tree oil that Melaleuca alternifolia growers and harvesters were exempted from military service until a sufficient surplus had been established.

After World War II ended a new wave of synthetic drugs grew to prominence. Penicillin and other antibiotics became the choice of doctors in treating every kind of infection. Synthetic chemicals were also developed to clean and disinfect wounds. The new synthetic medications were touted as the next wave of miracle cures, and their use quickly spread worldwide. As a result, the supply of tea tree oil was greater than the demand, and many producers went out of business. The high cost of the oil and the difficulty in obtaining it caused many pharmacies and doctors to stop recommending it. Tea tree oil, along with many other proven natural healers, fell to the wayside and became virtually forgotten.

THE FINAL "DISCOVERY" OF TEA TREE OIL

During the 1960s, a wave of discontent with modern medicines began sweeping the United States. People interested in natural remedies rather than complex, synthetic drugs and invasive treatments began seeking out many of the forgotten healers. This included tea tree oil. As a result new tests were performed on tea tree oil to see if it indeed was a legitimate treatment.

During that time, tea tree oil was harvested exclusively from Melaleuca alternifolia trees growing in the wild. Skilled harvesters would venture into the thick groves with razor sharp machetes, chopping down the most robust stocks of the tree. The leaves were pruned from the branches and placed in large distilling vats. The steam from the boiling water caused the glands of oil within the leaves to burst. The oil would boil off, be collected and even bottled up for sale out in the swamp. This method, though slow and labor intensive, did meet the needs of the growing number of tea tree oil consumers.

There were a few problems, however. The biggest concern was the inconsistency in the quality of oil being harvested. There are two main ingredients that contribute to Melaleuca alternifolia oil's effectiveness. They are Terpinen 4-ol and Cineole. Terpinen 4-ol is the main antiseptic ingredient, while Cineole gives the oil its penetrating ability. If the oil lacks Terpinen 4-ol, it will not be effective in the treatment of infections. If it has too much Cineole, it can be irritating, especially to sensitive skin. The actual levels of these two components can vary from tree to tree. Oil was being sold that was both ineffective and caustic to skin.

In order to protect consumers and establish the credibility of tea tree oil, in 1967, the Australian Standards Association established an official standard for oil of Melaleuca. Acceptable quality oil would have at least 35 percent Terpinen 4-ol and no more than 10 percent Cineole. Every scientific test conducted to determine Melaleuca oil's effectiveness has been done on pure tea tree oil that meets these standards.

By the middle of the 1970s, tea tree oil had really begun making a name for itself, once again, outside the country of Australia. Plantations were developed to increase the supply of oil. Around the world, people experimented with the oil, discovering more and more uses. The results were passed on by word of mouth. Although unrecognized by the "mainstream" medical community, alternative healers, herbalists, and chiropractors touted its effectiveness.

During the 1980s, the demand for tea tree oil sharply increased. The small distilleries and plantations that existed in the remote swamplands could not keep up with the demand. As a result, larger plantations began springing up across Australia outside the swampy regions. Growers began experimenting with different seeds and different growing conditions to see if they could duplicate the quality of "bush oil" harvested from natural stands of trees. Many of their first attempts produced oil of a quality that was not up to the Australian standards.

In 1985, the Australian Tea Tree Oil Association, comprised of a number of growers and buyers, decided to lower the tea tree oil standards in order to allow some of the previously substandard oil to be sold. The tea tree oil industry needed the change to remain profitable during this developmental phase. The minimum Terpinen 4-ol content was lowered to 30%, and the maximum Cineole content was raised to 15%. In addition, manufacturers could blend Melaleuca alternifolia oil with other oils and sell it as pure oil as long as those content levels were met.

Many growers stayed true to the original tea tree oil standards, seeking to produce nothing but the finest oil available. Reputable companies refused to sell any oil that had been blended. Knowing there was no research confirming that blended oils were effective in treating infections, these companies did not want to soil tea tree oil's growing reputation. Many growers began more intensive research to improve the quality of "plantation grown" Melaleuca alternifolia oil. During the 1980s, annual oil production was between 15 and 20 million tons.

TEA TREE OIL TODAY

Today, annual production of Melaleuca alternifolia oil exceeds 300 million tons. Melaleuca alternifolia oil is sold worldwide by direct marketing companies, health food outlets, and is used by dozens of other companies as ingredients in a variety of cosmetic and personal care products. Many different factors have converged that have led to the growth of the tea tree oil industry.

First, over the past decade, extensive research has been performed on 100% Melaleuca alternifolia oil, and the results have been amazing. Tea tree oil has been shown to be an effective treatment for cuts, burns and abrasions. Tests have also confirmed its effectiveness in treating acne, dandruff, a variety of fungal and bacterial infections, boils, and numerous dental problems. As a result, more and more doctors and dentists are using tea tree oil in their practices and recommending it to their patients as well.

Second, there is a growing concern over the excess use of synthetic chemicals in today's society. Modern chemicals have been linked to cancer and birth defects. Many modern medicines don't work or have too many unwanted side effects. Natural products are no longer being viewed as absurd or backwards. Educated consumers are actively seeking natural ingredients for medicinal and cosmetic purposes.

Third, growers in Australia, in conjunction with the government, are actively seeking new and more efficient ways to produce higher quality oil. Growers are now producing oil with over 40% Terpinen 4-ol and Cineole levels at 3%. Breakthroughs in genetic engineering have opened up new avenues of research. To ensure the future of the tea tree oil industry, a multi-million dollar research facility has been established at The Southern Cross University in New South Wales. The center, known as the Australian Tea Tree Oil Research Institute (ATTORI), is entirely devoted to discovering everything there is to know about Melaleuca alternifolia oil. Everyone, from growers to sellers, is actively involved with improving tea tree oil quality.

Although tea tree oil has become quite popular, some words of caution need to be shared. In 1996, the International Standards Organization (ISO) drafted new specifications for "tea tree oil." The Terpinen 4-ol and Cineole levels remained identical to the Australian standards set in 1985. However, the ISO made it possible for other species of Melaleuca tree oil to be sold as tea tree oil, oven though "tea tree oil" had been synonymous with Melaleuca alternifolia oil since the 1920s. No other species of Melaleuca tree has an essential oil as powerful as the Melaleuca alternifolia tree.

Today, even the American Tea Tree Association allows blended oil to be sold as "pure tea tree oil." It is important that you make sure you are purchasing a good quality of 100% pure Melaleuca alternifolia oil. There are a few good companies that guarantee the quality and purity of the oil they sell. Check the label. If it doesn't have at least 35% Terpinen 4-ol and no more than 10% Cineole (the 1967 standard), don't buy it. ❦

Healthy Body

ABRASIONS

These injuries occur when your skin slides across coarse materials, such as concrete, gravel or asphalt. Washing the area gently, yet thoroughly, with *Antibacterial Liquid Soap* and cool water quickly reduces the pain. (Warm or hot water increases nerve stimulation and pain in most people.) Allow the stream of water to wash off all visible particulates. Pick out any embedded material. *Apply Triple Antibiotic Ointment* or *MelaGel* and allow to remain open to the air if possible. Otherwise, use a loose bandage saturated with *Triple Antibiotic Ointment* or *MelaGel* to prevent sticking. Repeat administration of *Triple Antibiotic Ointment* or *MelaGel* as frequently as needed for several days until the wound is adequately covered with a scab.

ABSCESSES

Abscesses are painful, pus-filled sacks of infection which can occur in or on any surface of the body. Begin drinking *Melaleuca Herbal Tea* in place of other liquids 3 to 4 times each day. Apply *T36-C5* to the abscess. To encourage drainage and drive the *T36-C5* into the wound, apply hot moist packs over the area. If the abscess can be lanced and drained, soak afterward in a solution of 1 oz *Sol-U-Mel* and 2 tbsp of Epsom salts in 1 quart of warm water. If the area is unable to be soaked, saturate a hand towel in the solution, wring it out, heat in a microwave for 1 minute then apply to the affected area for 10 minutes. Repeat every hour to speed draining. Apply *Triple Antibiotic Ointment* or *MelaGel*. If needed, cover with gauze to absorb any seeping fluid and keep the area clean.

ACHES & PAINS (MUSCLE) See *Muscle Strain*

ACID INDIGESTION, ACID REFLUX See *Heartburn*

ACNE

Acne results from an overproduction by the oil glands in the skin. These can dry and harden, forming blackheads, and may produce a local bacterial infection and pimples. Food allergies, hormone imbalances, stress, or toxicity can cause acne. Suspect food allergies and experiment with elimination diets or get tested by a physician. Minimize sugar. Drink 3–4 cups of *Melaleuca Herbal Tea*, hot or iced each day, in addition to the regular 8 glasses of pure water you should normally drink. Reduce fats to less than 20% of total calories. Perspire for 20 minutes each day, preferably from exercise, but sauna or steam baths work also. Shower while washing entire body with *Antibacterial Liquid Soap* or *The Gold Bar* and a soft wash cloth. For those who prefer bathing, always put 1 oz of **Sol-U-Mel** in the tub. Especially avoid eating cooked oils such as margarine and potato chips. Get 20 grams of fiber including **FiberWise** drink or bar daily. Take **Vitality Pack 4 Essentials** which includes **CellWise**, a broad-spectrum antioxidant which helps fight inflammation, and **Florify**, a probiotic. Probiotics protect your immune system and have been shown to fight acne bacteria. Take **Coldwater Omega-3** to reduce inflammation. **ProVex-Plus** is a potent antioxidant that helps protect and heal skin.

The **Clarity Clear Skin Essentials** was specifically developed for the prevention of acne. Consistent use of this system usually delivers clear skin. Wash skin with the **Clarity Foaming Cleanser**. Apply **Clarity Astringent**, then **Clarity Oil-Free Moisturizer**. For breakouts use **Clarity Acne Treatment Créme**. Use **Clarity Acne Spot Treatment** when needed away from home. Apply **T36-C5** to blackheads to clear plugged oil ducts. Apply **Renew Intensive Skin Therapy** afterward to keep moisture in skin and resist oil accumulation. Avoid dry brush or friction rubs with alcohol as this stimulates oil production. Get enough rest.

ADD & ADHD

Attention Deficit Disorder and Attention Deficit Hyperactive Disorder are found in children and adults who have a reduced attention span and variable pattern of behavior problems. Many clinical studies indicate that there is a link with dietary and environmental factors. Food and chemical sensitivities frequently play a role. Areas of the brain appear over-stimulated while others show reduced electrical activity. Simple sugar cravings and intolerance appear to also be indicated. Several studies indicate a link with essential fatty acid deficiencies within the brain.

Identify any and all foods, food additives, household cleaners, and synthetic substances shown to be reactive, and remove them from the child's environment. Convert your home to safe Melaleuca cleaning and personal care products. Reduce fried foods, cooked and rancid oils (potato chips, french fries, etc), sugar (including artificial sweeteners), and food colorings. Have a metabolic and nutritional physical exam provided by a certified clinician.

The following supplements, along with appropriate dietary changes, may be useful to help improve symptoms. The **Vitality Pack** with **Oligofructose Complex** to help maintain proper nutrition. (Children should take **Koala Pals**.) **Luminex** to maximize cerebral circulation. **ProVex-Plus** to reduce free-radical activity and help to reduce sensitivities to allergens. **Phytomega** contains omega-3 fatty acids, which are extremely important for proper brain function. Researchers have discovered a link between mood disorders and low concentrations of omega-3 fatty acids in the body. **CellWise** to help maintain cell structure in the brain, and **Sustain Sport** to help maintain blood sugar balance and reduce sugar cravings.

AIR PURIFICATION

The quality of the air you breathe in your home may be robbing you of good health. Convert your home to Melaleuca products, replacing toxic cleaning and personal care products with safer Melaleuca products. The outgassing of toxic vapors from both personal care and home hygiene products significantly increases air quality problems. Remove browning leaves from house plants immediately. Provide good drainage for house plants, and do not over-water. Change furnace and cooling air return filters monthly during extreme weather usage: Spray all filters and vents often with diluted *Sol-U-Mel*. To do a Melaleuca oil purge of your house 2 to 12 times a year, attach an inverted open bottle of *T36-C5* on the furnace intake filter. The high air volume will diffuse the entire contents of the bottle throughout your house over the next 12 to 36 hours (depending upon temperature and relative humidity). This treated air flows throughout all the rooms and helps stop the growth of bacteria, molds, fungus and viruses. Take *ProVex-Plus* when exposed to toxic substances.

ALLERGIC REACTIONS (ALLERGIES)

Skin rashes, itching skin, sore throat, runny nose, sinus congestion, eye irritation, headaches, and fatigue are common symptoms of allergy sufferers. While individuals vary in their degree of sensitivity to allergic substances, it is important to minimize discomfort and prevent complications such as infections. Many of the aromatic oils from *Melaleuca alternifolia* have local-acting anti-inflammatory and desensitization effects.

Always try to avoid the allergen when possible. Your physician can help you determine the substances you are reacting to and begin a program to gain permanent desensitization. Applying *T36-C5* directly to exposed skin reaction sites (hands, arms, legs, feet, scalp, neck, and abdomen area) usually neutralizes the local histamine reaction and reduces symptoms. A word of caution—do not apply any Melaleuca products near or in the eyes. *Renew Intensive Skin Therapy* or *MelaGel* can be applied afterwards to give long lasting protection. Soaking in a bath containing 1 oz of *Renew Bath Oil* (and 1 oz of *Sol-U-Mel* if infections are present) offers an added soothing effect.

Remember, allergies are the result of an unhealthy immune system, so maximizing your nutrition is essential. Besides eating wholesome foods, the *Vitality Pack* with *Oligofructose Complex*, *CellWise*, and *ProVex-Plus* give extra protection against allergies by providing antioxidants in the form of beta carotene, vitamin C, and vitamin E, citrus bioflavonoids, and proanthocyanidins. Antioxidants reduce histamine levels which cause the itching, rashes, and burning. The calcium in *Vitality Mineral Complex* often gives immediate relief from sneezing and general body aches during a reaction.

For both chronic and acute allergies/hayfever, many people find relief from *ProVex-Plus*. It may need to be taken at the rate of 1 capsule for every 50 lbs of body weight per day in order to provide the most relief and prevention of allergies.

ANXIETY

When a person gets excited there are several adrenal hormones that are released to combat the stress. Anxiety is a condition when these hormones are either set off randomly or they do not return to normal after stimulation. While adequate exercise and rest are vital, nutritional supplementation can also be beneficial. Menopause or PMS can induce anxiety in some women.

Good nutrition should include the *Vitality Pack* with *Oligofructose Complex* and *CellWise*, along with *ProVex-Plus*. Taking *ProvexCV* may also be wise, depending on your age. *Luminex* and *Sustain Sport* taken as directed can be very helpful. Hormonal fluctuations resulting in anxiety during times of PMS or menopause might improve when *EstrAval* is taken daily.

ARTHRITIS

Hot, red, painful and stiff swollen joints of the hands, wrists, elbows, neck, back, hips, and knees are common symptoms of arthritis. The best long-term treatment is the one that gets at the cause. Some cases of arthritis respond to reducing white sugar, white flour, nicotine, caffeine, and alcohol. Generally avoid cold temperatures to the affected joint. For osteoarthritis, take **Replenex Extra Strength** to help rebuild cartilage and restore normal joint function. For all forms of arthritis take **ProVex-Plus** to help reduce inflammation. **Coldwater Omega-3** with 660 mg DHA and 270mg EPA has been shown to reduce inflammation. Some forms of arthritis respond well to resting the joint, while other forms, such as osteoarthritis, respond to motion such as knitting. **Pain-A-Trate** and **T36-C5** can be applied to the affected area to achieve rapid relief of pain and stiffness. Taking the **Vitality Pack** with **Oligofructose Complex** and **CellWise** with each meal provides essential trace nutrients for reducing further injury and increasing healing. Since dehydrated joints ache, drink more liquids, including 2 to 4 cups of **Melaleuca Herbal Tea** per day.

ASTHMA

Congestion and restriction of the lungs causes labored breathing and wheezing and affects 1 of every 12 people. Many are small children. Although it is associated with airborne allergies, toxins, and occasional food sensitivities, improvement can occur by following a few simple suggestions. Identify and restrict all sensitizing substances (see *Air Purification*). Rid your home of all toxic personal care and home care products. Convert your home to Melaleuca products, beginning with the **EcoSense Laundry System**.

The inflammatory process involved in asthma produces damaging free radicals. Adults and teenagers should take **Vitality Pack**, **CellWise**, and **ProVex-Plus** which not only provides necessary vitamins and minerals, but also protects antioxidants. Children should take **Koala Pals** and **ProVex-Plus**. For reducing inflammation take **Coldwater Omega-3**. Get enough rest. If congestion exists, increase the amount of **ProVex-Plus** until you find a level that provides relief. Further relief comes from a vaporizer or humidifier with water plus 10 drops of **T36-C5** and 2 capfuls of **Sol-U-Mel**.

Adults can try adding 10–20 drops of Tabasco sauce (capsicum) in a few ounces of water and drinking it immediately before a meal to reduce congestion and thin mucous in the lungs. One drop of **T36-C5** on a cotton-tipped swab gently used to clean pollen and dust from each nostril before bed has helped many children.

ATHEROSCLEROSIS See *Cardiovascular Disease*

ATHLETE'S FOOT

Athlete's foot is a contagious infection caused by a fungus, and is generally found between the toes. The infected areas are covered by itching cracked skin. This fungus is spread in public locker rooms, swimming pools, and showers. As in most infections, prevention is the best treatment. Always wear shower sandals when in public showers, such as athletic locker rooms and swimming pools. Spray feet with **Body Satin Foot Spray** and apply **Dermatin Antifungal Creme** between toes and to bottoms of feet immediately after showering. **Body Satin Foot Scrub** and **Body Satin Foot Lotion** can also be used to cleanse and stimulate

---

NOTE: The information presented in this book is in no way intended as a substitute for medical counseling. Always consult your physician before starting any course of supplementation or treatment, particularly if you are pregnant or currently under medical care. Always read and follow product packaging directions and warnings.

improved circulation. Direct sunlight and air drying the feet after showering or swimming is also a helpful preventive measure. Take the *Vitality Pack* with *Oligofructose Complex*, *CellWise*, and *ProVex-Plus* or *ProvexCV* with each meal to optimize trace nutrients. Drink 2 to 3 cups of *Melaleuca Herbal Tea* daily.

To eliminate the athlete's foot, clean the affected area well with *Antibacterial Liquid Soap* and water. For a great foot soak add ½ tsp. *Renew Bath Oil*, ½ tsp *Sol-U-Mel* in 1 quart warm water and soak feet in this solution for 20 minutes morning and night for one week. Pat dry. Apply *Dermatin Antifungal Cream* as directed. Or apply *T36-C5* followed by *Renew Intensive Skin Therapy* or *MelaGel* each morning and night. If there is no improvement after one week, discontinue use and consult your physician. To help avoid infecting other family members, spray porcelain or tile shower and bathtub surfaces as well as bathroom floors with *Sol-U-Guard Botanical* disinfectant.

ATHLETIC INJURIES

Typical athletic injuries to all ages include pulled muscles, strained ligaments and tendons, bruises and muscle cramps. Take the *Vitality Pack* with *Oligofructose Complex*, as well as *ProVex-Plus* each day to optimize tissue strengthening nutrients. *CellWise* should also be taken. Of course all adults should be taking *ProvexCV* as well to support a healthy cardiovascular system. Take more *Vitality Mineral Complex* if you have muscle cramps after a workout. Eat an *Access Bar* 15 minutes before exercise to inhibit adenosine and open fat stores in the body for energy. *ProFlex* helps restore, repair, and strengthen muscle tissues, and helps provide energy. *Sustain Sport* can be mixed in your water bottle for continual replenishment of waning blood sugar.

Replenex helps reduce inflammation and preserves the health of joints, thereby promoting ease of movement. *Pain-A-Trate* should be in the equipment bag of every athlete. Regular application of *T36-C5* stimulates circulation to injured tissue. Immediate application of *Pain-A-Trate* to any closed injury will start the healing process. Ice is good for injured joints, muscles, tendons, and ligaments. Apply ice for no more than 5 to 10 minutes at a time. Longer treatment periods can actually cause frostbite or reverse the anti-inflammatory effect. Heat can cause problems so it should be avoided, in most cases, for the first 24 to 48 hours after an injury to bruised or pulled muscles. Chronic or untreated injuries that do not resolve should be seen by a physician trained to treat sports injuries.

ATTENTION DEFICIT DISORDER See *ADD & ADHD*

BAD BREATH See *Body Odor*

BED SORES

Also known as decubitus ulcers, bed sores are wounds that occur when people are bedfast or confined to a wheel chair. Healing begins at the outer edges and works inward when pressure is removed from the area. Apply *T36-C5* to any blanched skin areas before the sore begins. It can often be halted at this stage. If a sore is present, gently wash the area with a washcloth and *Antibacterial Liquid Soap* enriched with one capful of *Sol-U-Mel* in 1 quart of warm water. Apply *Triple Antibiotic Ointment* or *MelaGel*. Cover with loose gauze. Use minimum amount of tape. Repeat washing and *Triple Antibiotic Ointment* every 8 hours

---

NOTE: The information presented in this book is in no way intended as a substitute for medical counseling. Always consult your physician before starting any course of supplementation or treatment, particularly if you are pregnant or currently under medical care. Always read and follow product packaging directions and warnings.

until the wound heals. This can take from one day to several weeks depending upon the overall health of the individual.

NOTE: Bed sores should be taken very seriously in diabetics, persons on immune suppressive drugs, and those with leg ulcers due to poor circulation.

BEE & WASP STINGS

Bees are territorial creatures that defend their territory by injecting a powerful chemical, formic acid, into the intruder. Grab and yank the stinger out as fast as you can. Wash the area with *Antibacterial Liquid Soap* and cold water. Immediately apply *T36-C5* or *MelaGel* to stop pain and prevent secondary infection. Do not use any other home remedies, such as baking soda, with the Melaleuca products in this treatment. Reapply every 15 minutes until all signs and symptoms are gone. Four to six treatments may be necessary. Take *ProVex-Plus* immediately and continue for 24 hours.

NOTE: When a person is allergic to bee or wasp stings, this can be life threatening. The allergic person should carry an antidote kit containing adrenaline and benadryl. Administer this according to the directions before any other therapy. Shortness of breath or difficulty breathing, puffy or swollen throat or eyes, rapid heart rate, dizziness, or profuse sweating are signs of allergic reaction and can appear within 10 to 30 minutes after being stung. DO NOT DELAY. GET EMERGENCY HELP!

BENIGN PROSTATIC HYPERPLASIA (BPH)

As men age, and especially after "male menopause," testosterone is inefficiently utilized in the prostate gland. Physical trauma (sitting), stress, excessive animal fat intake, and nutrient deficiencies induce oxidation of testosterone into dihydrotestosterone. This causes the prostate gland to enlarge and become less functional. Slow or dribbling urination, difficulty starting urination, incomplete emptying of the bladder, getting up multiple times at night, and reduced sexual function accompany this condition. Almost one half of men over the age of fifty experience symptoms of BPH.

BPH does not indicate cancer and should be differentiated from this more severe condition. Get annual prostate exams after age fifty including the sensitive blood tumor marker for prostate cancer called PSA. Prevention is the best treatment. Regular hot baths seem to reduce the incidence of BPH. Native Japanese men have a lower incidence of BPH and other prostate problems due to their custom of very hot baths. Americans tend to shower and have a statistically higher incidence of most prostate problems. The ingredients in *ProstAvan* have a proven effect in helping prevent BPH and should be taken every day by men over the age of forty. One extra tablet for every decade past forty is advised. *Luminex* is advised to maximize cerebral circulation and hormone regulation. the *Vitality Pack* with *Oligofructose Complex*, *CellWise*, and *ProVex-Plus* is also vital. Three cups of *Melaleuca Herbal Tea* each day is also helpful.

BLACK EYE

Bruising almost anywhere on the head can cause a black eye. Apply an ice pack as soon as possible after the injury, to slow down facial swelling. Do not use any Melaleuca products near the eye, as its aromatic vapor is drying to the eye and causes pain. Take the *Vitality Pack* with *Oligofructose Complex* as well as *ProVex-Plus* to speed healing and prevent easy bruising.

BLEEDING GUMS

Deep plaque or periodontal infections can cause bleeding gums, swollen gums or dental pain. Switching to Melaleuca dental care products often gives relief from bleeding gums. Regular brushing with *Whitening Tooth Polish* and rinsing with *Breath-Away Mouth Rinse* is a good way to control the build up of bacteria causing plaque. Daily flossing with *Classic Dental Floss* can clean between teeth where a brush cannot reach. If brushing after a meal is inconvenient, use *Exceed Sugarless Gum* to help remove loose food particles and kill bacteria. Drinking 2 to 4 cups of *Melaleuca Herbal Tea* per day helps promote a healthy environment in the mouth. Take the *Vitality Pack* with *Oligofructose Complex*, *CellWise*, and *ProVex-Plus* while eating a healthy diet. Get professional dental care if bleeding, pain, or swelling of gums persists.

BLISTERS

Friction, chemical, or heat injuries can cause blistering which may lead to blood poisoning if not properly treated. Do not puncture blisters. They can easily become infected. Nature's bandage is the best. Immediately apply *T36-C5* to a developing blister. Ice is often helpful also. This will usually prevent further development. If the blister has formed, apply *MelaGel* or *Triple Antibiotic Ointment* and a cushioned bandage. The fluid pressure should reduce within 6 to 12 hours. Repeat treatment daily until the overlying skin sags, breaks open on its own, and is replaced by a non-sensitive layer of skin from below. Continue treatment as long as there is pain, swelling, or redness.

BODY ODOR

Bacteria, yeast, bowel putrefaction, dental disease, vaginitis, chronic tonsillitis, kidney or liver dysfunction as well as a number of chronic degenerative disorders and chemical exposures can lead to a foul body odor. Drink 2 to 4 cups of *Melaleuca Herbal Tea* each day for detoxification. Take the *Vitality Pack* with *Oligofructose Complex* regularly. Brush regularly with *Whitening Tooth Polish*, floss with *Classic Dental Floss*, and use *Breath-Away Mouth Rinse* after meals. Use *Hot/Cool Shot Breath Spray* before going out in public, and chew *Exceed Sugarless Gum* frequently. If you are a smoker, STOP! Bathe instead of showering. Use *Antibacterial Liquid Soap* and *The Gold Bar* lavishly. Use *Body Satin Deodorant* after bathing and frequently during warm weather. Women can use *Nature's Cleanse* to douche weekly if needed. Pass the "odor test" from someone in your family before you use perfumes and colognes. When serious health concerns are causing the body odor, consult your physician. Take *ProVex-Plus* daily.

BOILS

Boils are raised, red, hard, hot, and extremely painful pus-filled skin abscesses caused by Staphylococcus organisms. Staphylococcus is very infectious and many strains are becoming resistant to prescription antibiotics. Apply *T36-C5* every hour to a developing boil. Some boils can be stopped at this stage. Leave exposed to the air if possible. When a focal head begins to appear, usually after a couple of days, use a sterilized needle to lance the boil and allow drainage. The release of pressure usually provides immediate relief of pain. Continue applying *T36-C5* as long as drainage lasts. If possible, soaking the site in a solution of 1 oz *Sol-U-Mel* and 2 tbs Epsom salts in a quart of hot water can speed drainage. Then apply *Triple Antibiotic Ointment* to a soft gauze bandage and cover. Drink 2 to 6 cups of *Melaleuca Herbal Tea* each day. Take the *Vitality Pack* with *Oligofructose Complex* with every meal. Take *ProVex-Plus* daily. If redness and swelling does not disappear after seven days, see your physician.

BRUISES

Ruptured blood vessels near the surface of the skin or in muscles can occur from injury, infection, or blood disorders. The immediate application of ice to a traumatized area helps reduce bruising. *Pain-A-Trate* has a deep penetrating effect and reduces swelling, increases circulation, and speeds healing. Apply as often as needed until pain, discoloration, and swelling disappear. *T36-C5* can be used on the bruise if *Pain-A-Trate* is not available. If the bruise injury is near the eye, use caution to not get the oil in or too near the eye. To prevent easy bruising and to speed healing, take *ProVex-Plus* or *ProvexCV* daily. These supplements improve the strength and elasticity of blood vessels.

BUNIONS

A bunion is a hard swollen area on the foot and is usually caused from ill fitting shoes. The swelling of the second synovial joint bursa produces enlargement and displacement of the big toe, which eventually laps over the second toe. Apply *T36-C5* or *Pain-A-Trate* generously to the affected joint as often as discomfort exists. Soak in a solution of 1 oz *Sol-U-Mel* and 2 tbs of Epsom salts per quart of hot water each night. Wear only well fitting shoes, and see your local chiropractor for a walking gait analysis.

BURNS

No burn is simple to treat! This is true for a first degree burn which is red and swollen, a second degree burn which produces a blister, or a third degree burn which penetrates into muscle and deep tissue and occasionally chars the flesh.

Always protect your skin from sunburn by using *Sun Shades Mineral Plus SPF 30+ Sunscreen*. Use *Sun Shades After Sun Hydrogel E* after a day in the sun to instantly cool overexposed skin, reduce redness, and soothe dryness.

Keep a bottle of *T36-C5* in the kitchen for treating grill and fryer burns. The oil provides an anesthetic-like action and alleviates most pain on contact. Immediately flush a fresh burn with cold water or apply ice and continue until the area is cold. Pat dry and apply *T36-C5*. Then cover with a thin coat of *Renew Intensive Skin Therapy*. Take *ProVex-Plus* daily to speed recovery and reduce scarring. Most first-degree burns will subside very soon. Repeat the *T36-C5* and *Renew Intensive Skin Therapy* application every hour until pain is gone.

For second-degree burns apply *T36-C5* immediately to prevent blistering. Repeat application of *T36-C5* and *Pain-A-Trate* each hour until pain and swelling are gone. If the burn does not show signs of healing, seek medical care.

Third-degree burns require professional care immediately, since deep blood vessels, nerves, and lymphatic vessels in the skin are damaged. After cold application, apply *T36-C5* and *Renew Intensive Skin Therapy* or *Triple Antibiotic Ointment*. Cover with a sterile covering. Contact your doctor immediately.

BURSITIS

Inflammation of small fluid-filled shock absorbing sacs, called bursa, causes swelling and painful movement of the joint, usually a shoulder, elbow, hip or knee. Take *ProVex-Plus* to help reduce inflammation. Apply *Pain-A-Trate* generously to the affected area every 2 to 4 hours. Moist heat and limiting joint motion may be helpful during the healing phase. Do not exercise the joint until pain and swelling are reduced. Seek medical advice if the pain does not subside in a few days.

CALLUSES

Thickening of normal skin caused by friction, usually on the hands or feet, is seen in people whose work causes repeated pressure on a particular area. Eliminate undue pressure to the affected site. Wear softer and better-fitting shoes. A moleskin or foam rubber protective bandage or arch inserts often help. *MelaGel* and *Renew Intensive Skin Therapy* applied regularly helps to prevent friction at the active site. *Body Satin Foot Scrub* and *Body Satin Foot Lotion* can also be used to cleanse and stimulate improved circulation.

CANCER PREVENTION

Cancer is the second most common life-threatening condition in North America, next to heart disease. Prevention is still the wisest strategy. Here is a formula which many scientists agree is reasonable for preventing this dreaded disease as well as most chronic degenerative illnesses: Optimum diet, plenty of exercise and rest, positive attitude, and a lifelong practice of prevention.

Whether or not you have had cancer, the recommendations included here can give you a greater measure of future cancer prevention. Many cancer researchers now believe that a combination of approaches to prevent cancer will prove to be the best treatment. Study your family tree for patterns of specific cancer types. Breast, colorectal, skin, prostate, uterus, and lung cancers seem to be more hereditary linked. Tobacco (cigarettes, pipe, smokeless tobacco), fatty diet (animal or cooked vegetable oils), toxic chemical exposure (household cleaners, personal care products, food additives, pesticides, herbicides, etc.), electromagnetic radiation (x-rays, TV, ultraviolet, etc.), and putrefying food in our digestive tract are the greatest known risks.

Get annual wellness checkups from a preventive physician. New blood tests (PSA for prostate, etc.) are being developed to detect antigens (immune sensitive chemicals) given off by early forms of cancer. Follow the doctor's recommendations.

Remove all sources of chemical exposure from your environment (especially household chemicals), and reduce your exposure to electromagnetic radiation as much as possible. Eat as if your life depended on it, because it does! Take the *Vitality Pack* with *Oligofructose Complex*, *CellWise*, and *ProVex-Plus* or *ProvexCV* to ensure adequate antioxidants, B vitamins, and essential trace

---

NOTE: The information presented in this book is in no way intended as a substitute for medical counseling. Always consult your physician before starting any course of supplementation or treatment, particularly if you are pregnant or currently under medical care. Always read and follow product packaging directions and warnings.

minerals, all of which are associated with cancer prevention.

To help prevent colon cancer, increase your fiber intake by eating a *FiberWise* bar for a quick snack or drinking the excellent *FiberWise* drink. Also research indicates that the ingredients in *Florify* may help to prevent cancer of the colon along with all of the other healthful benefits of maintaining a proper balance of flora in the intestines.

Men should take *ProstAvan* which contains lycopene, a nutrient found to reduce the risk of prostate cancer. Drink plenty of pure water and *Melaleuca Herbal Tea* to continually detoxify. Apply *T36-C5* or *Triple Antibiotic Ointment* immediately to any suspicious skin lesion, mole, wart, skin tag, or discoloration. Continue application 2 to 4 times each day until it disappears (probably 2 to 3 weeks) or until seen by your physician. Laugh, sing, and play at least 30 minutes each day.

CANKER SORES

Mouth ulcers, known as canker sores, form on the gums and the inside of the cheeks. Brushing with *Whitening Tooth Polish* and rinsing with *Breath-Away Mouth Rinse* reduces the bacterial count in the mouth. At the first sign of a canker sore, apply *T36-C5* to the injured site. Repeat every 4 hours.

See also the section on *Cold Sores*.

CARDIOVASCULAR DISEASE

Hardening of the arteries can lead to high blood pressure, shortness of breath, strokes, cold hands and feet, as well as senility and premature aging. Oxidized cholesterol (LDL—the bad kind) and ionic calcium make up part of the "cement" which lines arteries of the liver, bowel, lungs, brain, kidneys, legs and arms. Several common-sense suggestions can help:

Take *ProvexCV* daily as recommended to inhibit LDL cholesterol oxidation, regulate blood platelet activity, and maintain healthy blood pressure. Take *Phytomega* daily as recommended. The phytosterols and omega-3 fatty acids will help to lower cholesterol levels and maintain healthy triglyceride levels. Stop smoking and avoid smokers. Have a thorough physical examination performed to determine your risks. Follow the doctor's recommendations and chart your progress. Avoid animal fats and cooked vegetable fats. Reduce total fat to less than 20% of your total diet. Eat two green, yellow, and orange-colored vegetables each day. Take the *Vitality Pack* with *Oligofructose Complex* and *CellWise* as directed. Begin a gradual exercise program. Eat an *Access Bar* 15 minutes before exercising to speed up the fat-burning process. Add fiber to your diet to promote cardiovascular health. *FiberWise* contains 5 grams of fiber and the bars can be carried for a quick snack.

CARPAL TUNNEL SYNDROME

Those who use their hands with a continual repetitive motion experience a thickening of the nerve sheath in their wrists causing numbness, coldness and often pain. First, eliminate the repetitive motion that caused the problem until healing is completed (often 4 to 12 weeks). Take the *Vitality Pack* with *Oligofructose Complex* with every meal. Take the saturation dose of *ProVex-Plus* by taking one capsule for every 50 pounds of body weight for two weeks. Then gradually reduce the dose until a maintenance level is reached. In addition, take **Replenex** or **Replenex Extra Strength** as directed. Apply **Pain-A-Trate** to the inside of the wrist and outside of the elbow every 4 hours to reduce inflammation and control pain. Avoid cold water. Hot water gives temporary relief.

CHAPPED LIPS

Wind and cold takes its toll on mucous membranes of the lips. Cracking and pain can be prevented and lips restored to normal within 1 to 12 hours by applying **Sun Shades Lip Balm** every 15 to 30 minutes. **MelaGel** can also be used to speed recovery.

CHICKEN POX

Chicken pox is a common contagious disease of children. The symptoms can be treated by applying **T36-C5** directly on the vesicles. After the rash has fully developed, usually within 2 or 3 days, soaking in 1 oz of **Sol-U-Mel** and 1 oz of **Renew Bath Oil** in a tub of warm water for 15 minutes can help the itching. Drink one to four cups of **Melaleuca Herbal Tea** daily.

CHIGGERS

Chiggers are the larva of harvest mites that live mainly in the South and Midwestern states. The larva bore into skin pores and hair follicles to feed, causing a rash and itching. Rub **T36-C5** on the area of the bites each morning and evening. Follow by applying **Triple Antibiotic Ointment** to prevent secondary infection. Large areas can be treated by soaking in a warm tub with 1 oz of **Sol-U-Mel** and 1 oz of **Renew Bath Oil** while scrubbing with a wash cloth and **Antibacterial Liquid Soap**. For prevention, apply **T36-C5** to the bottom of pant cuffs, or spray pants and socks with 1 oz **Sol-U-Mel** diluted with 7 oz of water.

COLD SORES

Very painful clear, fluid-filled eruptions on the border of the mouth, forming hard, oozing scabs result from an infection of either the herpes simplex or herpes facialis virus. These cold sores may be started by a fever, a cold, a sunburn, or stress. Since the virus feeds on an excessive intake of the amino acid arginine, diets avoiding citrus fruit and nuts should be followed. Supplementation with the amino acid L-Lysine, found in most health food stores, is advised to stop the early spread of the infection. Dab **T36-C5** on the lesions immediately upon detection. Repeat every hour until the lesion either disappears or comes to a head. If it comes to a head, continue to apply **T36-C5** once every 2 hours followed by **MelaGel** or **Renew Intensive Skin Therapy**. For persistent or large surface sores, use **Triple Antibiotic Ointment** every 4 hours. See also the section on **Canker Sores**.

COMMON COLD

Cold viruses attack the moist, cooler regions of the nose, throat, sinuses, vocal cords, and larynx when our systems are run down. The common cold usually gives a warning that it is about to develop. From the earliest signs of tiredness, sneezing, and hoarseness you are given a few hours to launch an attack. Immediately take **Activate Immune Complex** as directed, and take a hot bath. Take **CounterAct** cold and flu medicines as directed. **CounterAct Cough Drops**

NOTE: The information presented in this book is in no way intended as a substitute for medical counseling. Always consult your physician before starting any course of supplementation or treatment, particularly if you are pregnant or currently under medical care. Always read and follow product packaging directions and warnings.

are formulated with menthol and Melaleuca oil to reduce coughs and sore, dry throat, as well as vitamin C to help boost the immune system. Also breathe the steamy vapor of 5 drops of **T36-C5** and water in a steam inhaler for 15 minutes (air temperatures above 104 degrees kill the virus). Apply one drop of **T36-C5** to each nostril of your nose every 4 hours. Sip vegetable broth and/or mom's chicken soup every couple of hours. Avoid temptation to eat heavy foods as your digestive tract, including smell and taste, are on vacation for awhile. If coughing is present, use **CounterAct Cough Relief Medicine** as directed. Try a hot **Sustain Sport** drink to fight any fever you may produce. "Drown the cold" with **Melaleuca Herbal Tea**—1 cup per hour. Use **Renew Bath Oil** as a chest and neck rub to boost your immune system, and bathe with it to reduce painful muscles. Get all the rest you can. Take the **Vitality 4 Essentials** which includes the **Vitality Pack**, **CellWise** and **Florify**, a probiotic. Probiotics have been shown to reduce risk and duration of colds and flu.

CORAL CUTS

Coral cuts often are jagged and irregular and harbor bacteria. This necessitates thorough cleansing with pure water and **Antibacterial Liquid Soap** enriched with **Sol-U-Mel**. Remove particles of sand and coral. Apply **T36-C5** or **T40-C3** for maximum disinfecting. Suturing wounds that cut through the skin and into muscle speeds healing and reduces secondary infection. Apply **Triple Antibiotic Ointment** over the stitches, if applicable, and cover with a gauze bandage. Daily inspect the wound for redness or swelling, which gives indication of the spread of infection. When sutures are not needed, soak affected areas in a solution of 1 oz **Sol-U-Mel**, plus 1 oz **Renew Bath Oil**, plus ¼ cup Epsom salt in 1 quart of hot water. Rinse open wounds daily with 1 oz of **Sol-U-Mel** in 1 pint of water. Change the dressing daily and reapply **Triple Antibiotic Ointment** or **MelaGel**.

CORNS

Corns are raised areas of hyperkeratosis or thick callused skin which are the result of ill fitting shoes causing friction or pressure over a bony extension of the foot, such as the ball of the foot or the toe joints. Soak feet in a solution of 1 oz **Sol-U-Mel** and 1 oz **Renew Bath Oil** in 1 quart of hot water for 15 minutes. Proceed twice daily until the corn softens enough to remove the core with tweezers. Apply **Triple Antibiotic Ointment** or **MelaGel** and cover with a small bandage. **Body Satin Foot Scrub** and **Body Satin Foot Lotion** can also be used to cleanse and stimulate improved circulation. Wear only shoes that fit properly.

COUGHING

Our bodies produce phlegm and mucous in the throat and lungs when exposed to severe temperature changes, chemical irritation, or allergens. We instinctively cough to remove this phlegm and foreign substances. Smoking is the most common cause of chronic coughs. Treat the cause—eliminate your exposure to the irritating substances. In mild cases, breathe the vapor of 5 drops of **T36-C5** in a bowl of steaming water for 15 minutes while holding your head over the bowl. Make a tent over your head and the bowl with a bath towel. Repeat morning and evening. Drink **Melaleuca Herbal Tea** throughout the day. Use **CounterAct**

Cough Relief Medicine as directed. *CounterAct Cough Drops* are formulated with menthol and Melaleuca oil to reduce coughs and sore, dry throat, as well as vitamin C to help boost the immune system.

CRAMPS

Sudden decreases in tissue oxygen, in muscle and nerve calcium levels, or hormonal changes before menstrual flow can trigger muscle cramps. Side aches during or after strenuous exercise are due to diaphragm spasms caused from low oxygen and low calcium levels in that muscle. Wait 45 minutes after eating a meal before exercising. Properly stretch and warm muscles before exercise. *Vitality Mineral Complex* taken 4 times per day and at bedtime can prevent sub-optimum levels of calcium in the blood and prevent cramps. Eat an *Access Bar* 15 minutes before exercise. Drink *Sustain Sport* during and immediately after exercise. A warm bath and a good massage can help reduce pain greatly. Massage *Pain-A-Trate* into muscles which cramp easily. The therapeutic dose of *ProVex-Plus* (1 capsule for every 50 pounds of body weight per day) can also give good relief, as can *CounterAct Extra-Strength Acetaminophen* or *Ibuprofen.*

CUTICLES

Dry cuticles, which split and become infected, are often due to exposure to harsh soaps or solvents such as gasoline or paint thinner. After washing hands with *Antibacterial Liquid Soap* or *The Gold Bar*, apply *Moisturizing Hand Creme* to the hands and work into the cuticles to prevent dryness. Apply *Triple Antibiotic Ointment* or *MelaGel* to infected cuticles. If condition persists, see your physician.

CUTS

Cuts should be treated soon after injury. Clean the affected area with a wash cloth, warm water, and *Antibacterial Liquid Soap* and/or *Sol-U-Mel*. Pat dry and apply *T36-C5* followed by *MelaGel* or *Triple Antibiotic Ointment* and keep clean with a bandage. Check the healing progress daily. Re-clean and apply new bandages as often as needed. Deep or wide cuts may require a visit to your physician for suturing.

DEPRESSION (MILD)

One of the most common conditions experienced by adults and young people is occasional depression—an attitude that "I don't feel like doing what I normally would like to do." It is normal for someone to feel blue or have an attitude of melancholy from time to time due to undesirable situations. It is another thing to see a black cloud cast over the future. Some people actually develop a sort of regular "gloom and doom" attitude if depression is allowed to persist. Nutritional deficiencies or fast foods often provoke such feelings. Exposure to household chemicals and food additives may also contribute. If a cause for the depressed mood can be identified, then the cause should be treated. Menopause can also increase the need for estrogen stabilization to control mild depression.

Nutritional research indicates that low levels of omega-3 fatty acids in the nervous system correlates with a higher risk of depression. Try adding

Phytomega or *Coldwater Omega-3* and *Florify*. Studies show that probiotics greatly reduce anxiety and depression. Unfriendly bacteria in the gut produce brain toxins. Good bacteria like those in *Florify* crowd out the bad bacteria. *Unforgettables* support memory, concentration and recall. Take *Luminex* along with the *Vitality Pack*, *ProVex-Plus* or *ProvexCV* and *CellWise*. *Estraval* can be taken as directed to reduce mild depression during the change of life.

DIAPER RASH

Common diaper rash is caused by friction and irritation in the presence of moisture, which triggers yeast to grow. This occurs naturally when wet diapers are not changed promptly. Properly launder all baby clothing as well as diapers with *MelaPower* enriched with 1 capful of *Sol-U-Mel* per load. *Sol-U-Mel* should not be used in babies' bath water as the green soap in it may irritate sensitive skin (newborn babies lack active sweat glands.) *Antibacterial Liquid Soap* or *The Gold Bar* should be used to bathe your baby. After towel drying your baby, allow skin to air dry (in direct sunlight if possible) for a few minutes. Apply *Renew Intensive Skin Therapy* to form a natural moisture barrier on the skin before diapering.

DIARRHEA

A sudden increase in stool volume, fluidity, or frequency of fecal excretion is seen with microbial infections, flu viruses, stress, food poisoning, laxatives, certain genetic and malabsorption problems, and electrolyte loss from vomiting or drugs. The greatest concern is depletion of body fluids. Children under the age of 4 can dehydrate quickly and die from uncontrolled diarrhea.

Determine the cause, if possible. If there is abdominal pain, fever, or if the diarrhea does not resolve rapidly, seek emergency help without delay. Otherwise begin drinking *Melaleuca Herbal Tea*, 4 to 16 ounces every hour along with *Sustain Sport* for energy and nutrient replacement. The probiotics in *Florify* have proven to be an effective treatment for diarrhea in children, travelers' diarrhea, lactose intolerance, and irritable bowel syndrome. Take as directed.

DISINFECTANTS

Disinfectants work by selectively reducing the population of disease-causing germs to make room for the friendly germs without harming humans or household plants and animals.

Sponge-bathe a sick person with *Antibacterial Liquid Soap* or *The Gold Bar* on a wash cloth to reduce surface germs often transported through perspiration. Rinse well. Disinfect the air by running a warm steam vaporizer with 10 drops *T36-C5* and 2 capfuls of *Sol-U-Mel* in the sick room. For preventing the spread of germs through the skin, use *Clear Defense Hand Gel* or *Wipes* throughout the day to sanitize and kill germs on hands without the need for soap and water.

To help prevent the spread of germs in the home or office, spray surfaces with *Sol-U-Guard Botanical*, a broad-spectrum disinfectant that is 99.99% effective against common kitchen and bathroom germs. In addition to bathroom and kitchen nonporous surfaces, also spray doorknobs, telephones, light switches, toys, etc. *Sol-U-Guard Botanical* is also EPA-approved for use in hospitals, day cares, schools, and nursing homes.

DRY SKIN

Some people have dry skin due to hormonal or nutrient deficiencies, prescription medications, or a deficiency of essential fatty acids in their diet. Hands that work in caustic or cold environments or those that are washed frequently (food handlers or health care workers) will develop excessively dry, cracked skin. Wash in *Antibacterial Liquid Soap*, then apply *Renew Intensive Skin Therapy* liberally. Apply *Triple Antibiotic Ointment* or *MelaGel* to cracked or infected areas. *Moisturizing Hand Creme* can be used on hands after washing to help restore moisture. When hand chapping has begun, apply *Renew Intensive Skin Therapy* every 4 hours until normal skin moisture is restored. Skin dryness that has invaded deeper tissues or caused swelling will require treatment with *Triple Antibiotic Ointment* every 4 hours. This will help to control infection until healing is accomplished. *Pain-A-Trate* has been used by some patients with poor circulation. Take the *Vitality Pack* with *Oligofructose Complex* with every meal, and take *ProVex-Plus* each day to help improve skin suppleness and elasticity.

EARACHES

You do not have to have infection to have earaches. Determine the cause of the pain, if possible. Cover a child's ears when out in cold or windy weather to prevent earaches. Loose cotton pushed into the outer ear canal can help protect sensitive ears. Holding the open end of styrofoam cups firmly over the ears when landing an airplane has a dramatic effect on preventing earaches in adults as well as children. A drop of *T36-C5* or *T40-C3* mixed with 15 to 20 drops of warm olive oil will help minimize pain. Insert the oil mixture directly into the outside ear canal with a dropper 3 or 5 times per day. Avoid using undiluted oil as local irritation can result. Melaleuca's *Sugarless Gums* contain xylitol. Xylitol's natural bacteria fighters, along with the act of chewing and swallowing, help clear a congested ear. If congestion exists, use *CounterAct* cold and flu medicines as directed.

EAR INFECTIONS

Repeated ear infections with fever and pain requiring cycles of antibiotics are a sign of continual blockage of the ear canal. Don't overlook allergies as a cause. Identify the cause, if possible. See your physician if in doubt. (**NOTE:** The American Lung Association cites formaldehyde as a possible major cause of chronic ear infection in children. Formaldehyde is an ingredient in many cleaning and personal care products commonly found in the home.) Never send a child with an ear infection outdoors if the air is cool.

To treat an ear infection use a drop of *T36-C5* or *T40-C3* mixed with 15 to 20 drops of warm olive oil. Insert the oil mixture directly into the outside ear canal with a dropper 3 to 5 times per day. Avoid using undiluted oil as local irritation can result. Xylitol gum can be very effective in preventing ear infections by inhibiting bacteria. Melaleuca's Sugarless Gums contain xylitol. Xylitol's natural bacteria fighters, along with the act of chewing and swallowing, help clear a congested ear. A hot water bottle or heating pad set on low should be put over the ear. Drink 4 to 16 ounces of *Melaleuca Herbal Tea* every hour to prevent dehydration from the fever. If congestion exists, use *CounterAct* cold and flu medicines as directed.

ENLARGED PROSTATE See *Benign Prostatic Hyperplasia (BPH)*

FEVER BLISTERS See *Cold Sores*

FLU See *Influenza*

FUNGAL INFECTIONS

Fungal organisms belong to the plant kingdom and are found on all healthy skin. Many infections are caused by opportunistic forms of fungi that take advantage of a person's weakened immune system. Fungal infections fail to respond to antibiotics but can successfully be treated with Melaleuca oil. Fungal infections have different names depending on the area of the body affected:

Skin *(Tinea corporis)* - See *Ringworm*
Feet *(Tinea pedis)*   -   See *Athlete's Foot*
Nails *(Tinea ungium)* - See *Ringworm*
Scalp *(Tinea capitis)* - See *Ringworm*
Groin *(Tinea cruris)* - See *Jock Itch*

GERMAN MEASLES See *Rubella*

GINGIVITIS See *Bleeding Gums*

GOUT

Painful joints of the toes, fingers, or other areas, along with elevated blood uric acid is typically known as gout. Sharp urate crystals cause physical damage to the cartilage. Once known as a "rich man's disease," gout affects those who are usually overweight, consume alcohol, large quantities of red meat and rich foods. Have a thorough physical examination performed and begin following the doctor's recommendations. Start a low stress diet consisting of more vegetables (a "greens and beans diet") and fewer animal products. Take **Replenex** to help rebuild damaged cartilage. Drink 2 to 4 cups of **Melaleuca Herbal Tea** each day. Apply **Pain-A-Trate** to any affected joints 2 to 4 times each day at first, then each morning and evening until painless mobility is achieved. Take a hot soak with 1 capful **Sol-U-Mel** in 1 quart of water 30 minutes each morning to minimize damage to cartilage.

GUM DISEASE See *Bleeding Gums*

HALITOSIS See *Body Odor*

HAY FEVER

Hay fever is one of the most commonly seen conditions. Its seasonal symptoms of tree, weed, and grass pollen hypersensitivity include runny, red and itching eyes and a runny, stopped-up nose. When possible, avoid exposure to the pollens you are allergic to. Due to cross sensitivity, food allergies may reinforce pollen allergies. For example, eating wheat may aggravate a wheat pollen allergy. The flavonoids in **ProVex-Plus** have been shown to have an antihistamine action as well as an anti-allergic action, so take at the rate of one capsule for every 50 pounds of body weight daily. This can be in addition to your daily **ProvexCV**

NOTE: The information presented in this book is in no way intended as a substitute for medical counseling. Always consult your physician before starting any course of supplementation or treatment, particularly if you are pregnant or currently under medical care. Always read and follow product packaging directions and warnings.

intake. Each night before retiring, swab each nostril of your nose with a cotton-tipped applicator containing *Renew Intensive Skin Therapy*. This will reduce the accumulated pollen from the day and moisten dry mucous membranes. Take the *Vitality Pack* each meal to boost your immune system. To stop hay fever attacks try a few sprays of *Hot/Cool Shot Mouth Spray*. A bit of *MelaGel* or *Sunshades Lip Balm* under your nose can act as a pollen barrier. See also *Allergies*.

HEAD LICE See *Lice*

HEARTBURN

Heartburn, also known as acid indigestion, is characterized by a burning sensation in the upper chest. It occurs after eating, bending over, or lying down. Normally, the lower esophageal sphincter (a muscular valve) opens just to allow food to pass into the stomach, however when it opens too often or does not close tight enough, heartburn is experienced because the stomach acids seep into the esophagus. Heartburn relief can be achieved through lifestyle changes. Eat dinner earlier; wait at least two to three hours before going to bed after eating. Eat smaller meals more often during the day. If you are overweight, losing weight may have a significant effect on your heartburn. Keep a diet diary/heartburn log to identify your trigger foods. Upon experiencing heartburn pain, take *Calmicid* as directed. For regular, frequent heartburn, try *Calmicid AC Acid Reducer*. It works by making stomach fluids less acidic and less irritating. *Calmicid AC Acid Reducer* goes to work within minutes and lasts 10 to 12 hours. Chew *Exceed Sugarless Gum* after meals and before bed to reduce sleep-related acid reflux.

HEART DISEASE See *Cardiovascular Disease*

HEMORRHOIDS

Hemorrhoids are varicosities of the veins of the hemorrhoidal plexus in the anus, often accompanied by inflammation, reddening, and bleeding. Hemorrhoids bother over 50% of adults. Preventing this condition is best. Get adequate exercise and water each day. Take *ProVex-Plus* each day as recommended. *FiberWise* drink or bars should also be taken every day to prevent constipation. A cotton ball or 2 x 2 inch gauze pad soaked with *T36-C5* or *Pain-A-Trate* held in the anal opening can quickly reduce the itching and burning. *MelaGel* applied to the area can also bring quick relief.

Chronic hemorrhoids are best treated as follows. Add 1 oz of *Sol-U-Mel* and 1 oz of *Renew Bath Oil* to 1 quart of warm water. Sponge the solution onto the hemorrhoidal area. Leave for several minutes. Pat dry. Apply *MelaGel* or *Triple Antibiotic Ointment*. Repeat the procedure morning and night for seven days. A hot sitz bath each evening with the above solution may be very helpful in shrinking any external hemorrhoids. Stubborn hemorrhoids may require conservative therapy beyond the use of Melaleuca products. Contact your physician about non-surgical hemorrhoid treatment.

HIVES

Hives are a form of skin rash that consists of raised white welts mixed with red patches on the skin. The cause of hives is an allergic or hypersensitive reaction.

Determine the source and avoid it in the future. The flavonoids in **ProVex-Plus** have shown to have an antihistamine action as well as an anti-allergic action, so take **ProVex-Plus** at the therapeutic dose of 1 capsule for every 50 pounds of body weight per day until relief is found. This can be in addition to taking your **ProvexCV** every day as recommended. Application of **T36-C5**, **MelaGel**, **Pain-A-Trate**, or soaking in a warm bath with 4 oz of **Sol-U-Mel** and 4 oz of **Renew Bath Oil** usually returns normal circulation to the affected area. Drink **Melaleuca Herbal Tea** 2 to 4 times each day to assist in detoxification. Chronic hives can be due to an underlying disease and should be brought to the attention to your physician. Of course, nothing stops the itch of hives like **DermaCort**. It is an anti-itch cream formulated with the #1 pharmacist-recommended itch-stopping ingredient, hydrocortisone, plus Melaleuca oil.

HOARSENESS

Hoarseness is due to inflammation of the voice box (larynx) and can be caused from simple overuse, such as yelling at an athletic event, or other disorders such as viral or bacterial infections. Inhale steam made from adding 10 drops of **T36-C5** and 2 capfuls of **Sol-U-Mel** to the water in a steam vaporizer. Drink hot **Melaleuca Herbal Tea** 2 to 6 times each day. Resting the voice usually reduces the symptoms within a few days and prevents further inflammation. For serious cases, seek medical attention.

HOT FLASHES

Menopausal aged women frequently experience sudden hot spells with profuse perspiration during the day or night. Adrenal-pituitary "storms" create an unstable hypothalamus which brings about inadequate thermal regulation. Insomnia and resulting anxiety can be a complication. Busy lifestyles and inadequate rest intensifies the general symptoms. Reduced stress is vital for control of hot flashes. Avoid sugar, caffeine, red meat (arachadonic acid), and chocolate. Use cold-pressed olive oil as a salad dressing. Get enough rest (night sleep and mid-day nap) and aerobic exercise. Take **EstrAval** and **Luminex** as directed. Maintain proper nutrition including the **Vitality Pack** with **Oligofructose Complex**, **CellWise**, and **ProVex-Plus**. Also enjoy 2 to 4 cups of **Melaleuca Herbal Tea** daily.

INFLUENZA (FLU)

Influenza is an infectious disease caused by a virus. Its many symptoms may include chills, fever, cough, headache, aches in the joints, weakness, and stomach distress. Much more severe than the common cold, the flu can progress to total exhaustion, acute bronchitis, pneumonia, and sometimes death. Upon the first signs of the flu, immediately take **Activate Immune Complex** as directed. Start drinking a cup of **Melaleuca Herbal Tea** every hour. Drink hot **Sustain Sport** to prevent exhaustion. Use **CounterAct Cough** as directed. Use **CounterAct Cough Drops** to reduce coughs and sore, dry throat. Use **CounterAct** cold and flu medicines as directed. Go to bed. Use **Calmicid** if indigestion or gas is present. Begin a steam vaporizer with 10 drops of **T36-C5** and 2 capfuls of **Sol-U-Mel** in the infected person's room. Take **ProVex-Plus** as directed, and **CellWise** every 2 to 4 hours for the antioxidant effect which reduces pain of muscles, chest, and abdomen.

INGROWN TOENAILS

Ingrown toenails are usually due to poorly fitting shoes. One method of preventing a recurrence is to file a "V" notch on the middle of the nail so that the point nearly touches the quick. This will cause the nail to draw towards the center and prevent the embedding of the edges of the nail. Trimming in a rounded fashion is not recommended as this actually causes further ingrown toenails. If possible, carefully remove the ingrown part of the nail. Soak the foot for 15 minutes in a solution of 1 oz *Sol-U-Mel* per quart of hot water. Dry thoroughly. Apply *T36-C5* followed by *MelaGel* or *Triple Antibiotic Ointment*. Repeat morning and night. *Body Satin Foot Scrub* and *Body Satin Foot Lotion* can also be used to cleanse and stimulate improved circulation.

If there is an infection, see the section on *Abscesses* in this book.

INSECT BITES

Most plagues and life-threatening communicable diseases have had biting insects (or other families of bugs) as carriers. From the fleas carrying black plague throughout Europe to the malaria-carrying mosquito that took the life of Alexander the Great, insect bites should not be taken lightly. Many unexplained itches and tiny sores on sleepers have been due to nocturnal flying and crawling bugs attracted by body heat. These insects can remain dormant in an unattended dwelling for years awaiting their next (or first) meal.

When staying in a cabin or beach house, immediately fumigate the area with 10 drops of *T36-C5* in a pan of boiling water. The insect repellent properties of Melaleuca oil are international—this works anywhere. Apply *T36-C5* to children's clothing or spray with diluted *Sol-U-Mel* when going to natural parks or walking in the forest in the spring. Mix a few drops of *T36-C5* in *Renew Intensive Skin Therapy* or *Moisturizing Hand Creme* to spread over the skin.

Inspect your children and yourself daily for small breaks in the skin indicating bites. If you discover an attached tick upon your inspection, cover it in *T36-C5*. The tick should soon let go, and you'll be able to remove it easily. Apply *T36-C5*, *MelaGel*, or *Triple Antibiotic Ointment* and cover with a bandage for 24 hours.

INSOMNIA

Insomnia is a condition characterized by the inability of a person to fall asleep or by wakefulness in the middle of the night. Some of the possible causes are a stressful lifestyle, indigestion, over-excitement, pain, discomfort, coffee or other stimulants, or drugs.

General good health is the best approach in preventing insomnia. Avoid caffeine, nicotine, alcohol, sugar, and a sedentary lifestyle. Regular daily exercise, deep breathing, drinking most liquids early in the day, and practicing a philosophy that lives life in one-day segments are good habits to ensure good sleep. A relaxing walk after dinner helps digestion and promotes good sleep.

Take *Calmicid* if heartburn, acid indigestion, or gas are present. Taking the *Vitality Pack* with *Oligofructose Complex* and *CellWise* as directed and *Sustain Sport* drink while being active will prevent the body from becoming imbalanced in neurohormone production.

ITCHING & FLAKING SKIN

Itching and flaking skin can be caused by several different health concerns. Those suffering from psoriasis or allergies can experience itchy and flaky skin. This condition may also be seen in people whose diet is deficient in essential oils and some who are post-menopausal. Bathe with **Renew Bath Oil**. Wash with **The Gold Bar**. Apply **Moisturizing Hand Creme** or **Renew Intensive Skin Therapy** to troubled areas. **Sun Shades** protects and moisturizes skin. Take **ProVex-Plus** to help restore skin suppleness and elasticity. See your physician for further instructions.

JOCK ITCH

Fungal infections of the groin, commonly known as *Jock Itch*, can form ring lesions around the sides of the crotch. Scratching of the area can cause secondary infections or chronic dermatitis. Bathing in 1 oz of **Sol-U-Mel** and using the **Antibacterial Liquid Soap** or **The Gold Bar** is helpful in controlling the fungus. Pat dry and apply **Dermatin Antifungal Creme** as directed. **T36-C5** and **MelaGel**, or **Triple Antibiotic Ointment** are also effective. **Renew Intensive Skin Therapy** may be used at bedtime. If irritation occurs, or if there is no improvement, discontinue and consult your physician.

LEG CRAMPS

Leg cramps are due to either a deficiency in circulating calcium or reduced oxygen to muscles. Muscle cramps tend to appear after unconditioned physical activity. Stretching a "crampy" muscle can prevent knotting. Exercise in 3 steps: warm up for 5 minutes to stretch muscles, do your work out, then cool down by moving slower until the heart returns to its pre-exercise rate. Eat an **Access Bar** 15 minutes before beginning exercise. Take the **Vitality Pack** and **CellWise** as directed. Drink **Sustain Sport** before, during, and after exercise to reduce stress on the body. Persons who are bedridden may need the assistance of external pneumatic compression boots to maximize circulation and prevent leg pains.

LICE

Lice are small parasitic insects that feed on the victim's blood. Immediately upon suspecting or seeing evidence of lice, shampoo with **Melaleuca Original Shampoo** and bathe in a tub of water with 1 oz of **Sol-U-Mel** and 1 oz of **Renew Bath Oil** added. Afterward, massage **T36-C5** into scalp and hair to soften and dislodge the nits (the eggs of the lice). Don't be stingy with the oil! Comb the oil through the hair. To fumigate the live insects, wrap your hair in a hot moist towel for 10 minutes. Repeat every second day for at least 5 treatments (10 days). To avoid reinfection, wash all clothing and bedding with **MelaPower** laundry detergent plus **Sol-U-Mel** in hot water. Add 2 oz of **Sol-U-Mel** to 16 oz of water and spray the entire house, especially affected areas. As a preventative measure mix 3 drops **T36-C5** and 3 drops of lavender oil with water in a 4 oz spray bottle. Shake well and spray on hair before brushing. Use on dry hair once a day.

MACULAR DEGENERATION

Macular degeneration is the deterioration of the central focal region of the back of the eye called the macula, resulting in impaired vision. Take **NutraView**, which promotes long-term macular health and visual acuity with lutein, bilberry, blueberry, and Vitamin C. Take the *Vitality Pack* and *CellWise* as directed. Take *ProVex-Plus* daily to promote vascular integrity, also *Vitality Coldwater Omega-3* to help reduce inflammation. If you are older than 60, get a visual field evaluation test performed by your eye doctor each year.

MEASLES

Rubeola, also known as red measles, is a highly contagious viral infection characterized by fever, bronchial cough, sneezing, and irritated eyes that are sensitive to light. A brownish-red rash starts around the ears, on the face and neck, then spreads over the trunk and occasionally the limbs, and usually lasts 4 to 7 days. In well-nourished children and adults, measles usually passes without complications. In malnourished or unhealthy individuals, great care must be taken to prevent a weakened immune system. Preventing ear infections (see *Ear Infections*), bacterial infections (see *Disinfectants*), and pneumonia is a primary goal. To prevent respiratory complications, use a warm steam vaporizer in the person's room with 10 drops *T36-C5* and 2 capfuls *Sol-U-Mel*. Drink *Melaleuca Herbal Tea* 3 to 6 times each day.

MOUTH ULCERS See *Canker Sores*

MUCOUS

Thin, watery mucous is a product of healthy membranes in the body and is needed to protect soft tissues from damaging environmental substances. Thick, discolored or stringy sputum (phlegm), vaginal, eye, stool or nasal mucous is a sign of irritation or infection. Mild bacterial growth, viruses, chronic yeast or fungal infections, digestive problems, stress, allergies and chemical sensitivities can produce this type of mucous. Drink 2 to 6 cups of *Melaleuca Herbal Tea* each day to reduce the number of harmful organisms in the bowel and urinary tract. Use *CounterAct Cough Relief Medicine* as directed. If congestion exists, use *CounterAct* cold and flu medicines as directed. Breathe steam and *T36-C5* to clear nasal, and sinus mucous membranes. Douche with *Nature's Cleanse* as directed to reduce vaginal viruses, yeast, molds, fungus, and bacteria. Repeat any of the above to maintain healthy mucous.

MUSCLE CRAMPS See *Cramps* or *Leg Cramps*

MUSCLE STRAIN

There are several levels of muscle strain. Mild strain occurs regularly with all forms of exercise. Severe muscle strains can cause tearing and bruising. Overused muscles, tendons (connecting muscles to bones), and ligaments (connecting bones to other bones) are helped by immediately applying ice to prevent swelling. Keep the ice on for 5 to 10 minutes each hour, until the swelling is reduced. *Pain-A-Trate* gives dramatic relief from athletic strains. Soaking in a hot bath with *Renew Bath Oil* is very relaxing for aching muscles.

OBESITY

The underlying causes of clinical obesity (being more than 20% above your optimum weight, or having more than 40% of your body weight as fat) often stems from boredom eating, stressful eating, childhood or sexual abuse, drug effects, or improper nutrition. Less than 10% of obesity involves glandular conditions. The obvious problem is in storing more calories than are being burned through metabolic need and exercise. All chronic degenerative diseases are accelerated when obesity is present.

See your health care provider and begin following his/her advice. Start with a high-fiber, low-fat diet. Lots of fiber cleanses the body, removes toxins, and helps to dilute, bind, and deactivate many carcinogens. It moves excess bile from the stomach and intestine, prevents obesity, lowers cholesterol, stabilizes blood sugar, and increases energy. Use *FiberWise* drink or bars regularly to increase the fiber content in your diet. Take *Florify* to maintain a proper balance of flora in the digestive system.

Eat an *Access Performance Bar* 15 minutes before exercise. This will allow your body to actually burn stored fat. Melaleuca's online tool to encourage, inform, and challenge you to meet your exercise and diet goals is *Vitality for Life* at **www.vfl.com**. There are step-by-step exercise and meal recommendations, as well as the community support of your peers in the online forums. Plan your meals ahead of time. Remove all unhealthy snack foods from your home. Enjoy *Attain* as a healthy meal replacement. It is especially effective for weight loss when it is mixed with water or rice milk. *Attain* can also be mixed with *ProFlex20* for added protein. Protein helps lower appetite cravings and cholesterol while it increases strength and endurance. *Attain* is a great replacement for *Slim Fast* and *Ensure*. *Luminex* would be helpful in boosting the level of 5-HTP, which is known to help in obesity.

OSTEOARTHRITIS See *Arthritis*

PARONYCHIA
Paronychia is an infection of the tissues around a fingernail or toenail. The infection may follow the nail margin and may extend beneath the nail where the infection penetrates more deeply into the finger or toe. Early detection and treatment is important. Wash the affected area with *Antibacterial Liquid Soap* and soak for 15 minutes in 1 quart of warm water and 1 oz of *Sol-U-Mel*. Pat dry. Apply *T36-C5* to the fingernail or toenail morning and night, then follow with *Triple Antibiotic Ointment* or *MelaGel*. Cover the area with a loose bandage. Chronic infections may require repeated applications for several months. If Candida albicans is the causative agent in a female, douching with *Nature's Cleanse* may be needed to reduce the source fungus. Drink *Melaleuca Herbal Tea* 2 to 4 times each day.

PERIODONTAL DISEASE See *Bleeding Gums*

PIMPLES See *Acne*

POISON IVY, POISON OAK, POISON SUMAC
Complex chemical agents in certain plants are capable of producing acute dermatitis in sensitized individuals. Poison ivy, poison oak, or sumac's blistery rash is a result of coming in contact with the plant itself, or handling the clothing of someone who has. Immediate removal of the affecting agent is necessary

for any treatment to be effective. Immediately wash the area thoroughly with *Antibacterial Liquid Soap* and warm water. Pat (don't rub) dry. Apply *Triple Antibiotic Ointment* or *DermaCort* and cover with a loose gauze bandage three times each day until resolved. If the rash or blistering has appeared before treatment can be started, soak gauze bandages in cool *Melaleuca Herbal Tea* and cover the affected area. Re-soak gauze and apply every 15 minutes until pain subsides. Draining the blisters can be done, but do not remove the covering skin. If pain does not reduce, apply *Pain-A-Trate*. Contact your physician if improvement is not seen after 4 days.

PROSTATE See *Benign Prostatic Hyperplasia (BPH)*

PRURITIS ANI

Pruritis Ani is Latin for "itching anus." Itching around the anus can be caused from something as simple as pin worms in children, or as complicated as rectal cancer in adults. Many causes stem from chemical irritation with perfumed soap or toilet tissue. Food allergies (particularly eggs or milk) are frequently associated with this condition and often produce a red ring around the anal opening. Try to treat the cause. Soaking in a warm bath with 1 cup of Epsom salt and 1 oz of *Renew Bath Oil* often reduces anal muscle tightness which contributes to the itch. Avoid applying or consuming chemical conditioned substances. Take *Florify* to help maintain the proper balance of flora in the digestive system and combat Candida overgrowth. Drink 2 to 6 cups of *Melaleuca Herbal Tea* each day. Take the *Vitality Pack*, *CellWise*, and *ProVex-Plus* as directed. *Pain-A-Trate* can be dabbed around the anus during extreme cases to minimize itching. *Renew Intensive Skin Therapy* often gives lasting relief from pruritus ani while the true cause is being corrected. If itching persists, consult your physician.

PSORIASIS

Psoriasis is a chronic and recurrent disease of the skin that is characterized by dry, well-circumscribed silvery scaling patches of various sizes. The cause is unknown, but it appears to be related to inadequate detoxification, possibly through the kidney or the alimentary tract. Bathe using *Antibacterial Liquid Soap* and soak in *Renew Bath Oil* for 30 minutes each night. Pat dry (don't rub). Apply *Renew Intensive Skin Therapy* to the scaly areas. Apply *T36-C5* to newly inflamed or red areas. Cover with *MelaGel*. Daily sunlight exposure for 15 to 20 minutes is helpful. Practice relaxation. Eat healthy food. Take the *Vitality Pack* with *Oligofructose Complex*, *CellWise*, and *ProVex-Plus* as directed and drink 2 to 6 cups of *Melaleuca Herbal Tea* daily. Taking *FiberWise* can aid in detoxification. *Coldwater Omega-3* helps reduce inflammation. Consult your physician for further advice.

RASHES

Many things can cause rashes. They should be treated to prevent secondary infections and reduce any stinging or itching. Take a hot bath with 1 oz of *Renew Bath Oil*, plus 1 oz of *Sol-U-Mel*, and soak for 20 to 30 minutes. Pat dry. Apply *Renew Intensive Skin Therapy*, *Triple Antibiotic Ointment*, or *Pain-A-Trate* to the affected area. Of course, nothing stops the itch of a rash like *DermaCort*. It is an anti-itch cream formulated with the #1 pharmacist-recommended itch-stopping ingredient, hydrocortisone, plus Melaleuca oil.

RINGWORM

A round, reddened, often bull's-eye-appearing rash anywhere on the skin is evidence of ringworm. At least three different strains of fungi can cause ringworm. Household pets such as cats and dogs carry these fungi on their fur and skin. As in most infections, prevention is the best thing to stop the spread of the infection. Family members must take precautions to not pick up the infection from another family member. Always wear shower sandals when in public showers such as athletic locker rooms or in swimming pools where the fungi grow readily and cross with other strains. Bathe your cat and dog regularly with *Sol-U-Mel* during warm weather. Treat any pet rashes or "hot spots" with *T36-C5*, *Triple Antibiotic Ointment*, or *MelaGel*. See *Healthy Dogs & Cats*.

Bathing is advised over showering. Always put 1 oz of *Sol-U-Mel*, along with *Renew Bath Oil* in the tub. Use a clean washcloth with the *Antibacterial Liquid Soap* or *The Gold Bar*. Cracking or oozing skin should receive a generous amount of *Renew Intensive Skin Therapy*. Apply *Dermatin*, *T36-C5*, *MelaGel*, or *Triple Antibiotic Ointment* on any suspicious areas of the skin immediately after showering or bathing. Direct sunlight and thoroughly air drying the body after showering or swimming is a great preventive act also. Take the *Vitality Pack* with *Oligofructose Complex*, *CellWise*, and *ProVex-Plus* as directed to optimize trace nutrients. Drink 2 to 3 cups of *Melaleuca Herbal Tea* daily.

RUBELLA

Rubella (German Measles or Three-Day Measles) is much milder in children and adults than "red" measles. After 14 to 21 days from the time of exposure, susceptible persons will feel tired and may have slightly swollen lymph nodes under the eyes, behind the ears, and in the neck. Other symptoms include the development of a headache, moderate fever and runny nose and a fine textured pinkish rash which starts on the face and neck, moves to the trunk and limbs, and lasts about three days. Since the active virus can be spread from about one week before to one week after the eruption of the rash, epidemics of rubella sweep through susceptible children quickly. By then the virus has spread throughout the body. Only palliative care can be given to ease discomfort and prevent secondary infections such as pneumonia. Soaking in a hot bath with 1 oz of *Renew Bath Oil* and 1 oz *Sol-U-Mel* for 20 minutes may help diminish the rash. Chicken soup, *Melaleuca Herbal Tea* and *Koala Pals* children's multivitamin is the ration of choice. More solid food can be given upon request, which is usually after the rash subsides.

SCABIES

Scabies are transmittable parasitic infections characterized by intensive itching and secondary bacterial infections. They are caused by the itch mite known as Sarcoptes scabiei that burrows under the skin to feed and lay its eggs. The itching is usually noticed most intensely when the person is in bed. Soak in a hot bath for 20 minutes each night with 1 oz of *Renew Bath Oil* and 1 oz of *Sol-U-Mel*. Apply *T36-C5* to the affected areas each morning and night. Apply *Renew Intensive*

Skin Therapy or *Triple Antibiotic Ointment* to give long-term protection against infection. Apply *Pain-A-Trate* to extremely itchy areas. If no improvement is observed within seven days, contact your physician.

SCALDS

Hot water, steam, liquid nitrogen, or liquid propane can produce scalds. Immediate blistering and light colored skin is characteristic. Care should be taken to not dislodge delicate superficial skin. Painful blisters may appear within a few minutes indicating second degree penetration. Loose, swollen skin without blistering is evidence of third degree penetration. Immediately apply cold water to hot water scalds and warm water to cold scalds. Pat dry and apply *MelaGel*, *T36-C5*, or *Pain-A-Trate* to the affected area. Wrap area with a sterile dressing. Begin treating as a second or third degree burn.

SEBORRHEA

Seborrhea is a dry or greasy scaly inflammation of the skin, which occurs around the scalp, face, and occasionally other areas of the body. It is caused from toxicity and is often misdiagnosed as thick dandruff. Take the *Vitality Pack* with *Oligofructose Complex*, *CellWise*, and *ProVex-Plus* as directed. Drink 2 to 6 cups of *Melaleuca Herbal Tea* daily for detoxification. Bathe using *Antibacterial Liquid Soap* in a tub containing 1 oz of *Renew Bath Oil* and 1 oz of *Sol-U-Mel*. Shampoo with *Melaleuca Original Shampoo* daily. Continue the bathing procedure once daily, but apply *T36-C5* with either *Renew Intensive Skin Therapy* or *MelaGel* after each bath.

SHINGLES

Shingles are caused by the same virus in adults that causes chickenpox in children. Shingles manifests as small, very painful clusters of blisters that form along a sensory nerve on the skin of the chest, neck, face, stomach or limbs. Shingles can be treated similarly to chicken pox, except for the use of more *Sol-U-Mel* and *Renew Bath Oil*, detoxification, and satisfying the increased nutritional need for B vitamins. Take the *Vitality Pack* with *Oligofructose Complex*, *CellWise*, and *ProVex-Plus* as directed. Drink 2 to 6 cups of *Melaleuca Herbal Tea* to reduce virus growth. Add 2 oz of *Renew Bath Oil* and 2 oz of *Sol-U-Mel* to a warm tub of water. Soak for 30 minutes. Pat dry. Apply a drop of *T36-C5* to pustules followed by *Triple Antibiotic Ointment*. Continue treatment once or twice daily for six days. Consult your physician if further advice is needed.

SINUS CONGESTION

Sinus congestion can be due to mild infections or generalized irritations caused from allergies, chronic airborne pollutants, cigarette smoking, dust, grasses, pollens or other chemicals. Often, bacterial sinus infections are caused by repeated use of antihistamines that dry mucous membranes and lead to severe susceptibility to other infections. Drink 2 to 6 cups of hot *Melaleuca Herbal Tea* each day as a decongestant. (NOTE: For Adults Only. To ¼ cup of warm *Melaleuca Herbal Tea*, add ⅛ tsp of sea salt. From a cup, snort the mixture into your nose. Tilt your head back and hold it in your sinuses for 10 to 15 seconds. Expel the mixture through your nostrils into a sink. Blow your nose gently.

Repeat morning and evening.)

Use **CounterAct Cough Drops**, which contain menthol and Melaleuca oil, to reduce coughs and help open nasal passages. Dab **T36-C5** directly under each nostril. Breathe the enriched steam from a vaporizer or a bowl of very hot water each morning and night before bed. To do this, add 10 drops of **T36-C5** and 2 capfuls **Sol-U-Mel** to the water. Form a tent over your head and the vaporizer, breathing the aromatic vapors through your nose and mouth deeply and gently into your lungs. Keep your eyes closed. Add 1 or 2 drops of **T36-C5** every 5 minutes for 15 to 20 minutes. Repeat each morning and evening, or run the vaporizer all night. Apply **Pain-A-Trate** on the temples and forehead to reduce pain from the congestion. Repeat every 2 to 4 hours for relief. As long as congestion exists, use **CounterAct** cold and flu medicines as directed.

SORE GUMS

Damage to the gums from over-zealous brushing or flossing of the teeth, or from rough foods, needs immediate attention to prevent secondary infections and canker sores. Poor dental hygiene or accumulated plaque below the gum line can lead to periodontal infections. See your dentist or dental hygienist without delay. Following an injury, immediately swish your mouth with **Breath-Away Mouth Rinse**. Follow the printed directions. Apply **T36-C5** to the sore area with your finger or a cotton swab to reduce the soreness. Take **ProVex-Plus** to strengthen gum tissues, reduce inflammation, and to help reduce plaque buildup. Use the **Whitening Tooth Polish**. It combines the anti-bacterial properties of propolis and myrrh with Melaleuca alternifolia oil. Not only does it fight bacteria, which often is the cause of sore gums, but it also works against plaque buildup.

SORE THROAT

Viruses, bacteria, allergens, pollutants, prescription drugs, and overusing our voice can produce a sore throat. Many people get a sore throat if they do not get enough rest. Whatever the cause, proper treatment is necessary to prevent the condition from escalating. Upon the first signs of a sore throat, take **Activate Immune Complex** and continue until all symptoms are gone. Gargle with **Breath-Away Mouth Rinse** to reduce bacteria and viruses. Use **CounterAct Cough Drops** as needed to help relieve throat pain. Spray throat with **Hot/Cool Shot Breath Spray** as often as needed. If the soreness returns or does not diminish, consult your physician.

THRUSH (ORAL)

Thrush is a fungal infection of the mouth or throat, caused by the Candida albicans organism. Use **Breath-Away Mouth Rinse**, as directed, every 2 hours. Brush with **Whitening Tooth Polish**. Drink 2 to 6 cups of **Melaleuca Herbal Tea** daily. Take the **Vitality Pack** with **Oligofructose Complex**, **CellWise,** and **ProVex-Plus** with each meal. Avoid sugar, alcohol, yeast bread products, cheese, and vinegar products.

TICKS

Ticks thrive in a warm, moist environment. They are often found on dogs, cats, deer, or livestock, and may jump to a human host when given the opportunity. Inspect your children and yourself daily when any outdoor activity takes place.

Cover your hands to prevent disease contamination. If you discover an attached tick upon your inspection, use tweezers or forceps to gently grasp the head near the mouthparts and pull it out. Put the tick in a jar of rubbing alcohol for identification and watch for any symptoms of sickness in the victim for two weeks. Apply *T36-C5*, *MelaGel*, or *Triple Antibiotic Ointment* to the site where the tick was and cover with a bandage for 24 hours. If illness is noted within two weeks of the bite, bring the victim and the tick sample to the doctor immediately.

TOOTHACHE

Dental problems are more easily prevented than treated at home. A sensitive tooth, due to root exposure, thin enamel, or cavities can begin aching from things such as sweets, hot or cold foods, or an uneven bite plane. For prevention, brush with *Whitening Tooth Polish* and use *Breath-Away Mouth Rinse* after every meal. If brushing after a meal is inconvenient, use *Exceed Sugarless Gum* to help remove loose food particles and kill bacteria. Use *Whitening Dental Floss* at least once each day. Apply *T36-C5* with a cotton swab directly to the sensitive tooth and surrounding gum to achieve immediate relief and see your dentist to determine the cause of your pain. Have regular checkups with your dentist to maximize the general health of your teeth.

URINARY TRACT INFECTIONS

Almost any normal skin organism is capable of living in the nutrient rich, moist, and dark environment found in the lower urinary tract. Women are more prone to UTI's because of the constant moist environment of the urethral opening and its close proximity to the anus. If improperly treated, UTI's can progress to bladder infection (cystitis) or kidney infection (nephritis). The best treatment is prevention. Take *CranBarrier* Daily. Use cotton undergarments. Dry your body well after showering or bathing. Drink enough water and 4 to 12 cups of *Melaleuca Herbal Tea* each day. Take the *Vitality Pack* with *Oligofructose Complex*, *CellWise*, and *ProVex-Plus* as directed. Douche as needed with *Nature's Cleanse*. If results are not achieved with these suggestions, contact your physician for further advice.

VAGINITIS

Bacteria and yeast can infect the nutrient rich vaginal lining causing painful swelling, foul odor, colored discharge and reduced libido. For acute infections, use *Nature's Cleanse Feminine Douche* morning and evening for 3 to 5 days. For re-occurrences or chronic infections, douche each night. Bathe instead of showering each night, soaking for 30 minutes with 1 oz of *Sol-U-Mel* and 1 oz of *Renew Bath Oil* added to the bath water. Avoid sugar. Drinking 2 to 6 cups of *Melaleuca Herbal Tea* each day and 2 to 3 quarts of water per day, along with the *Vitality Pack* with *Oligofructose Complex*, *CellWise*, and *ProVex-Plus* as directed helps build resistance to infections.

VARICOSE VEINS

Enlarged veins in the lower legs are common among civilized people because of standing and walking on flat hard surfaces all day. Chronic constipation and pregnancy also tend to cause circulation back-up in the legs, which leads to varicose veins. Following these simple suggestions has helped many patients with varicose veins. Elderly people may require specialized care beyond these suggestions. The bioflavonoids in **ProVex-Plus** and **ProvexCV** have been known to greatly reduce the unsightly appearance of varicose veins, so take daily. Do not wear tight fitting belts or girdles. Wear support hose ONLY when walking or standing for prolonged periods of time. Wearing them while sitting or driving can cause more circulation problems than it helps. Walk barefoot for 10 minutes each morning in the dew or on a sandy beach! **Body Satin Foot Scrub** and **Body Satin Foot Lotion** can also be used to cleanse and improve circulation in the feet and lower extremities. Maintain healthy regular bowel movements—you should not have to strain when making a stool. Drink 2 to 6 cups of **Melaleuca Herbal Tea** each day and take one or two **FiberWise** bars or drinks each day for added bowel mobility. Take **Florify** to help maintain the proper balance of flora in the digestive system.

WARTS

Common warts, also known as verruca, are non-cancerous tumors caused by pathoviruses. Viral warts most frequently grow on the hands or fingers of children. The elbows, knees, face, and isolated sites elsewhere on the body are less common. They appear most frequently on sites subject to injury. Plantar warts are common on the sole of the foot. When they are flattened by pressure, they are surrounded by cornified tissue and may be very tender. **Body Satin Foot Scrub** and **Body Satin Foot Lotion** can be used to cleanse and improve circulation. For isolated common warts, apply **T36-C5** each morning and night faithfully for up to 3 weeks. If the wart is thick and dry, shave the excess away before applying **T36-C5**. For body warts, bathe for 30 minutes in a hot tub with 1 oz of **Sol-U-Mel** and 1 oz of **Renew Bath Oil** added. Apply **T36-C5**, **Renew Intensive Skin Therapy** or **MelaGel** afterward. Some warts require the added strength of **T40-C3** to disappear. A few warts do not respond to Melaleuca oil.

YEAST INFECTIONS

Yeast such as Candida albicans are naturally occurring in every human and do not tend to activate the body's immune defenses except in overgrowth situations. They are naturally kept from growing out of control by neighboring friendly bacteria that secrete anti-yeast chemicals. Broad-spectrum antibiotics given for other conditions innocently destroy these friendly bacteria. When the body is left unprotected by these friendly bacteria, yeast can have a picnic on the nutrient-rich protein found on the skin and sugar enriched mucous membranes. Once yeast infections get started, they must be dealt with in an aggressive way for best results. Use **Nature's Cleanse** according to the directions. Melaleuca alternifolia oil is the only antiseptic capable of eliminating each of the major types of vaginal yeast infections while exhibiting virtually no toxicity to vaginal tissue. Take **Florify** to help keep yeast and harmful bacteria in the digestive system in check. Drink **Melaleuca Herbal Tea** and take the **Vitality Pack** with **Oligofructose Complex**, **CellWise**, and **ProVex-Plus** as directed. Avoid sugar, yeast, or mold-processed foods. Apply **T36-C5**, **MelaGel**, **Triple Antibiotic Ointment**, or **Renew Intensive Skin Therapy** to affected areas other than the vagina. (See also *Vaginitis*.)

NOTE: The information presented in this book is in no way intended as a substitute for medical counseling. Always consult your physician before starting any course of supplementation or treatment, particularly if you are pregnant or currently under medical care. Always read and follow product packaging directions and warnings.

Healthy Home

IS YOUR HOME A HEALTHY HOME?

The first step in making your home a healthy one should be to eliminate as many toxic substances as possible, especially toxic chemicals in cleaning products. Household cleaning products are among the most toxic substances we encounter daily. In one study conducted over a 15-year period, women who worked at home had a 54% higher death rate from cancer than women who had jobs away from the home. The study concluded that the increased death rate was due to daily exposure to hazardous chemicals found in ordinary household products. A 1985 EPA report concluded that the toxic chemicals in household cleaners are three times more likely to cause cancer than outdoor air pollution. Many of these chemicals have been linked to allergies, asthma, birth defects, infertility, miscarriage, central nervous system disorders, ADD and other learning disorders. Another EPA report stated that indoor air pollution is one of the nation's most important environmental health problems.

If that's not bad enough, every year 1.5 million accidental ingestions of poisons are reported to U.S. Poison Control Centers. The majority of the victims are under the age of twelve and have swallowed a cleaning or personal care product.

Fortunately Melaleuca has made it easy for us to make our homes healthier and safer environments for our families. Begin by boxing up all of the toxic grocery store brand cleaning and personal care products you may still have. Please do not pour them down the drain as this causes a very serious environmental problem. Give them to a neighbor or friend who still uses grocery store brands. Replace them with Melaleuca's alternatives. You will still need to store them high in a locked pantry, as many are made with powerful natural substances and could still be harmful to a child if swallowed or spilled in the eye. Follow the cleaning suggestions in this section for best results.

If you would like additional information on the health effects of toxic household chemicals, there are two very fine booklets available on this important topic, *Let's Stop Poisoning Our Children!* and *Is Your Home a Healthy Home?* We also publish a video of a CBC news presentation entitled *Toxic Brew*. You may order from **RM Barry Publications** by calling toll-free **1 (888) 209-0510**, or by visiting **www.RMBarry.com**.

HEALTHY HOME

Solutions

AIR FRESHENER

To make a fresh smelling and safe air freshener, combine 3 oz of *Sol-U-Mel* with 16 oz of water in a spray bottle.

AUTOMOBILES

For dusting the inside, spray a solution of 1 tsp of *Tough & Tender* in 16 oz of water on a cloth. Wipe the area thoroughly. Alternatively try the *Tough & Tender Wipes* for the dashboard and other surfaces. For the windows, spray on *Clear Power* (diluted to ½ the strength suggested on the bottle) and wipe them with a soft cloth or cheap paper towels.

Rustic Touch cleans vinyl and leather. It is also great for cleaning the dash of your car. **NOTE:** Spray it on a cloth to apply. If you spray it directly on the dash, you will get it on the inside of your windshield.

For cleaning the outside of the car, fill a bucket with warm water and add 1 oz of *Tough & Tender*. Apply with a cloth or spray bottle, and rinse with clean water.

To clean under the hood of your car, mix 1 capful of *Sol-U-Mel* and 2 oz of *MelaMagic* in a 16 oz spray bottle and fill with water. After spraying it on, let set for 10 minutes and hose off the dirt and grime.

Add 4 to 5 drops of *Tough & Tender* to every 4 oz of water in your windshield washer. It works amazingly well. (Make sure to use non-freezing washer fluid in the winter.)

BABY WIPES

Combine 1 tsp of *Sol-U-Mel* OR 1 capful of *Nature's Cleanse* with 1 capful of *Renew Bath Oil*, ¼ tsp of *Tough & Tender* and 2 cups of water to make very effective and cost-efficient baby or travel wipes. Cut a roll of paper towels in half and remove the cardboard roll so that you can begin pulling the towels from the center. Place the towels in a plastic container and saturate with this solution. Replace the lid and cut a "star" in the center. You can then pull the towels through the lid.

An alternate solution would be to cut a roll of 1 ply (cloth like) Viva paper towels in half and place ½ of the roll into a 3 quart Rubbermaid Servin' Saver bowl with a lid. Add 2 cups of water, 1–2 tbsp of *Koala Pals Hair Wash* and 2 tbsp of baby oil. If you experience problems with mold developing, add 1–2 drops of *T36-C5* to the mixture. Cover and let them soak for 10 minutes or so before using. Remove the center cardboard core and pull wipes from center and tear off.

Another recipe for baby wipes would be to use white Bounty paper towels (because they are stronger), and cut the roll in half. Take out the cardboard core. Mix in a large bowl—2½ cups of warm water, 1½ tsp of *Tough & Tender*, ½ tsp of *Sol-U-Mel*, and 1 capful of *Renew Bath Oil*. Stir and then put the ragged edge of the paper towels into the water first. Let this set until all the water is soaked up. Put the towels into a large plastic container with a lid. Pull from the middle. This also makes wonderful hand and face wipes. Only half of a roll of towels is used, so make 2 bowls at once.

NOTE: Always read and follow product packaging directions and warnings.

BARBECUE GRILLS

Soak your barbecue grill in a solution of 1 oz of *MelaMagic* in ½ gallon of water. Clean it with a brush. For the outside of the grill, use ⅓ cup of *Tough & Tender* in a 16 oz spray bottle of water and scrub with a soft brush. For baked on areas, use the *Tough & Tender* solution and let soak for a few minutes before scrubbing and rinsing.

BATHROOM – COUNTER

Use *Sol-U-Guard Botanical* disinfectant to treat your bathroom surfaces. This will kill any germs that may be on your counter. **Never use** *Sol-U-Guard* **on natural stone surfaces.**

PreSpot works great on laminated countertops for tough stains. Spray it on and let it soak for a few minutes before wiping.

BATHROOM – DISINFECTING

Sol-U-Guard Botanical is a broad-spectrum disinfectant that is 99.99% effective against common bathroom and kitchen germs.

BATHROOM – FLOOR

Combine 2 tbsp of *MelaMagic* and 1 capful of *Sol-U-Mel* in 16 oz of water. Spray or wipe it on the floor and mop thoroughly.

BATHROOM – HARD WATER SPOTS

Mix ⅓ cup of *Tub & Tile* and 1 capful of *Sol-U-Mel* with water in a 16 oz spray bottle. Sprayed on hard water spots this solution will clean and shine, but also will wipe out fungus, mold, and mildew. **Never use** *Tub & Tile* **on marble or granite surfaces.**

BATHROOM – MIRRORS

Use *Clear Power* (diluted to ½ the strength suggested on the bottle). Wipe the mirror with the *Clear Power* and cheap paper towels.

BATHROOM – MOLD & MILDEW

Apply *Tub & Tile* full-strength. Spray it on and let it stand a few minutes before rinsing. This is also excellent when cleaning mold and mildew off bathroom shower curtains. **Never use** *Tub & Tile* **on marble or granite surfaces.**

BATHROOM – ODORS See *Odors*

BATHROOM – SHOWER CURTAIN

Combine 1 capful of *Sol-U-Mel* and 1 oz of *MelaMagic* with water in a 16 oz spray bottle and thoroughly spray the shower curtain. Allow some time for the cleaning combination to work and then use the shower to rinse off the mixture before wiping off the remaining grime.

BATHROOM – SHOWER STALL

Use *No Work Daily Shower Cleaner*. With *No Work* you can keep your shower sparkling clean with a daily 15-second spray. Its dual action breaks up soap scum and hard water deposits and leaves behind a fresh smell.

NOTE: Always read and follow product packaging directions and warnings.

BATHROOM – SINK

Mix 4 tbsp of *Tub & Tile* and 1 capful of *Sol-U-Mel* with 16 oz of water in a spray bottle. Spray the sink and wipe it with a damp cloth. For rust stains or mineral deposits, use *Tub & Tile* full-strength. You may need to use a soft bristle brush on stubborn stains. Rinse the sink with water. By the way, the *Whitening Tooth Polish* is a wonderful enamel cleaner. **Never use *Tub & Tile* on marble or granite surfaces.**

BATHROOM – TOILET

Pour 2 oz of *Tub & Tile* in the toilet. Let this set for a few minutes, and then clean the area with a toilet brush.

If you have a lot of buildup, turn the water off on your toilet and let it drain. Pour in 2 oz of *Tub & Tile* and let it set for a few minutes before scrubbing with a toilet brush.

Use *Sol-U-Guard Botanical* to disinfect the seat and exterior surfaces.

BATHTUB

Mix 3 oz of *Tub & Tile* with water in a 16 oz spray bottle. Spray on the tub and let it set for about 2 minutes. Wipe with a damp cloth. For rust spots, apply straight *Tub & Tile* to the area. Wait until the rust dissolves and then wipe with a damp cloth. For hard water or mineral deposits, use full-strength *Tub & Tile* with a soft scrub brush. Initially there may be strong fumes due to the quantity of build up being dissolved, so run the fan or open a window. This problem should disappear very soon if *Tub & Tile* is used on a regular basis. **Never use *Tub & Tile* on marble or granite surfaces.**

To maintain a cleaner tub, keep a bottle of *No Work* close by and spray the tub each time it is used.

For the chrome, try *Clear Power*. It is very effective.

BLEACH SUBSTITUTE See *Laundry–Bleach Substitute*

BLOOD STAINS See *Laundry Stains*

BUMPER STICKER REMOVAL

Old bumper stickers should disappear by applying concentrated *Sol-U-Mel*. Let soak for a few minutes. It may take a couple of applications before the glue is dissolved.

CAR CLEANING See *Automobiles*

CARPET CLEANER – MACHINE MIX

Check the color fastness of your carpet before using any cleaning product. Clean carpets by mixing 1 oz of *Tough & Tender* and 1 capful of *Sol-U-Mel* for each gallon of water in your cleaning machine reservoir. This makes an excellent carpet cleaning machine solution. If you have greasy or hard to remove stains, try 1 oz of *MelaMagic* and 1 capful of *Sol-U-Mel* per gallon. If you have soft water, reduce the amount of ingredients by at least 50%.

NOTE: Rinse your carpets well after steam cleaning or shampooing, as any remaining product will attract dirt.

NOTE: Always read and follow product packaging directions and warnings.

CARPET – DEODORIZATION

Mix 1½ capfuls of *Sol-U-Mel* with water in a 16 ounce spray bottle. Spray on the carpet and let it set for 5 minutes. Clean the carpet with a scrub brush and blot the area with a damp cloth.

CARPET – SPOTS

Clean spots on your carpet with 1 tsp of *Tough & Tender* and 1 capful of *Sol-U-Mel* blended in a 16 oz spray bottle filled with water. If the spot is greasy, try 1 oz of *MelaMagic* combined with 7-8 oz of water.

An alternate choice might be to mix 2 tbsp of *PreSpot* with ½ capful of *Sol-U-Mel* in a 16 oz spray bottle filled with water. Apply the solution to the soiled area. Let it set for 5 minutes and then clean it with a soft brush. Blot the spot with a damp cloth until it is clean.

For extremely difficult spots, try concentrated *PreSpot*. It may need to soak for a couple of hours before you rinse with warm water, but it usually does a good job and will not discolor the carpet.

CEILINGS

For a very effective general cleaning disinfectant, mix 1 tsp of *Tough & Tender* in a 16 oz spray bottle of water or add 1 oz of *Tough & Tender* to a gallon bucket of water. If you need a stronger mixture, add 1 capful of *Sol-U-Mel* to either the spray or the bucket.

CHEWING GUM

Remove all the chewing gum possible before applying concentrated *Sol-U-Mel*. Rub fabric against fabric or use a soft brush to clean the area.

ALWAYS check the color fastness of any carpet or fabric **BEFORE** applying *Sol-U-Mel* or any cleaning product.

COPPER

Have you tried the penny test to see what *Tub & Tile* does to copper? Dip a copper penny in a capful of *Tub & Tile* and watch it clean that dirty, tarnished old penny in seconds. It will do the same for your copper pots and frying pans. Spray or wipe *Tub & Tile* on the copper and wipe the grit and black tarnish away. In most cases it is not even necessary to use it concentrated.

CRAYON

To clean crayon marks off of walls, use concentrated *Sol-U-Mel*. Gently try a small amount on the crayon mark, as this may also remove what is under the crayon mark—such as the paint.

For clothing, spray the affected area with full strength *PreSpot*. Let it set for a few minutes. Scrub the mark to loosen the crayon from the fabric. If the spot still exists, repeat the procedure. When the crayon has been removed, wash the clothing with *MelaPower Laundry Detergent*.

DIAPERS

Most people use disposable diapers now, but for those who still prefer to use cloth ones, odor is sometimes a challenge. Be sure to use a pail with a lid for soiled diapers. Cover the diapers with a combination of water and 1 capful of *Sol-U-Mel*,

---

NOTE: Always read and follow product packaging directions and warnings.

1½ tablespoon of *MelaPower 6x* and 1½ tablespoon of *MelaBrite 6x*. Soak them overnight before washing with 1 tablespoon of *MelaPower 6x* (1 pump) and 1–2 capfuls of *Sol-U-Mel*. For whiter diapers, add 1–2 tablespoons of *MelaBrite 6x* as well. Treat the diaper pail regularly with *Sol-U-Guard Botanical* to disinfect.

DISINFECTANT

Sol-U-Guard Botanical is the first botanical disinfectant that's 99.99% effective against common germs. Spray wherever germs can be found—kitchen counters, food preparation surfaces, bathrooms, garbage cans, doorknobs, light switches, toys, phones, etc. **Never use *Sol-U-Guard* on natural stone surfaces, however.** Alternatively, mix a 1:5 solution of *Sol-U-Mel* to water as a disinfectant.

Remember to carry *Clear Defense Hand Gel or Wipes* with you everywhere. It can be used in restaurants, public restrooms and simply after handling doorknobs and shaking hands.

DISHES – DISHWASHER WASHING

When you first begin to use *Diamond Brite* in your dishwasher, run at least one empty cycle with 1 oz of *MelaMagic* and the regular amount of *Diamond Brite*. This will clean out any residue or buildup from the commercial soaps previously used. Then, use the *Diamond Brite* as directed. If you have soft water or a high efficiency dishwasher, you may need to reduce the amount of *Diamond Brite* by ⅓ to ½.

Clear Power is a very good replacement for the rinse cycle products. Add straight *Clear Power* to the dispenser and check for really sparkling glasses.

DISHES – HAND WASHING

Use 5 to 7 drops of *Lemon Brite* in a sink full of water. For baked-on food, fill a container with hot water to which 2 or 3 drops of *Lemon Brite* have been added. Let the dishes soak for ½ hour and then wash as usual.

DISHES – STAINS

Soak stained dishes or china in a bucket or sink of hot water containing ⅓ cup of *Diamond Brite*. Let them soak for 1 hour. If stains have not dissolved, soak them overnight.

DUSTING

Always dust before you vacuum so that the dust particles can be picked up by the vacuum cleaner. Keep your air conditioner and heater clean and well serviced so that the amount of dust and bacteria particles floating throughout your home is limited.

Using *Rustic Touch* will condition your wood furniture and woodwork, while it cleans dust and wax buildup and leaves behind a mirror shine. The cleaned surfaces stay non-magnetic and seem to repel dust and dirt for a longer period of time. Use it on natural and artificial wood furniture, laminated surfaces, vinyl, leather and paneling.

On all other surfaces, mix ½ tsp of *Tough & Tender* with water in a 16 oz spray bottle. Spray on a cloth and wipe away the dust. The *Tough & Tender Wipes* are pre-moistened biodegradable wipes great for dusting.

NOTE: Always read and follow product packaging directions and warnings.

FINE WASHABLES See *Laundry – Fine Washables*

FIRE ANTS

Spray the ants with *PreSpot*. It is very effective, and they won't come back! For fire ant pain, splash the area with *Sol-U-Mel*.

For a foolproof way to kill fire ants consider this: After you have mopped the floor with *Tough & Tender* and/or *MelaMagic*, or you have washed the car with *Tough & Tender*, add 5 or 6 drops of *Lemon Brite* and stir. Pour half of the bucket on the fire ant bed. After about 30 minutes pour the other half on the bed.

FLOORS – LINOLEUM & CERAMIC

For mopping, use 4 oz of *MelaMagic* in a gallon of water. For a quick clean up, make a spray by mixing 2 tsp of *MelaMagic* in a 16 oz bottle filled with water.

To kill bacteria and fungus on nonporous bathroom and kitchen floors use *Sol-U-Guard Botanical* disinfectant as directed.

FLOORS – HARDWOOD

Use 1 oz of *Tough & Tender* in a gallon of water to clean your hardwood floors. Be sure to dry the floors carefully.

FURNITURE

For spot cleaning of fabric, use 1 tbsp of *PreSpot* with 16 oz of water. (You may want to test for color fastness on a hidden area.) For wood, leather or vinyl, use *Rustic Touch* as directed.

GARBAGE CANS

Pour ¼ to ½ cup of *MelaMagic* and 1 to 2 capfuls of *Sol-U-Mel* into the garbage can. Fill the can ¼ full with hot water and scrub the sides with a soft brush. Pour the mixture out and rinse with water. To prevent odor, clean them frequently.

An alternate solution would be to use *Sol-U-Guard Botanical* as directed for extra-strength disinfecting power.

GLASS

Use *Clear Power* as directed on the label. Terry towels, old cloths or very cheap paper towels are excellent for wiping windows after spraying. (Try using the *Clear Power* diluted to ½ of the strength suggested on the bottle.) For best results use distilled water with the *Clear Power*. See also *Windows* in this chapter.

GRASS STAINS – CLOTHING See *Laundry Stains*

GREASE SPILLS

Pour full strength *MelaMagic* on the grease spot and let it set for 15 minutes. Then wipe it up.

GREASE SPOTS – RUGS & CARPETING

Rub a small amount of *Antibacterial Liquid Soap* into the spots on your rugs or carpeting for a quick cleanup. Rinse and blot the stain with a dry cloth.

GUM See *Chewing Gum*

NOTE: Always read and follow product packaging directions and warnings.

HARD WATER SPOTS

For heavy duty cleaning of hard water spots, rub the area with concentrated *Tub & Tile*. Rinse and wipe dry. Do not use *Tub & Tile* on marble surfaces.

HOT TUBS

No Melaleuca products, including *T36-C5*, *Renew Bath Oil*, or *Sol-U-Mel*, should be used in an operating hot tub or permanent Jacuzzi tub. Melaleuca alternifolia oil is not compatible with the filtration system in those sophisticated environments.

To clean an empty hot tub, use full-strength *MelaMagic* and it may require a lot of elbow grease, but it will work.

HUMIDIFIER

Placing 1 to 2 tbsp of *Sol-U-Mel* in your humidifier's water chamber will not only clean it but will fill your home with fresh, healthy air.

INK STAINS – CLOTHING & SURFACES

Spray *PreSpot* on ink stains and rub with your finger or a soft brush. Let it set for a few minutes and then rinse with warm water. If it is a stubborn stain, repeat the procedure or soak the spot overnight.

An alternate solution is to use *Tub & Tile* or *Sol-U-Mel* directly on the spot. *Sol-U-Mel* is especially effective if the fabric has been in the dryer before being treated. It may also be used on "dry clean only" fabrics.

Be sure to check all fabrics for colorfastness before applying any product.

For ink on surfaces, try rubbing the area with a combination of 1 oz of *MelaMagic* and 1 capful of *Sol-U-Mel* mixed in 8 oz of water. The ink should be easily removed unless the surface has not been sealed.

INSECT REPELLENT

To rid your home of creatures such as roaches, beetles, crickets, and termites, try treating them with 3 oz of *Sol-U-Mel* in a 16 oz spray bottle filled with water. Spray around baseboards, thresholds, kitchen cabinets, and anywhere you see bugs in the house.

The "ultimate" insect repellent consists of 4 oz of *Sol-U-Mel*, 4 oz of *Renew Bath Oil*, and 5 oz of *Moisturizing Hand Creme.* Spread on exposed skin or over the entire body. Keep in mind, shampooing with *Melaleuca Original Shampoo* also affords insect repellent protection.

Some prefer to simply use 1 tsp of *Moisturizing Hand Creme* with 5 drops of *T36-C5* spread over all exposed skin.

For a general outdoor spray, blend ½ oz of *Sol-U-Mel* in a 16 oz spray bottled filled with water.

Also note that *Tub & Tile* will kill wasps and *PreSpot* and *Tough & Tender* will kill ants.

KITCHEN – ALL PURPOSE CLEANER

For a general, all-purpose kitchen cleaner, add 1 tsp of *Tough & Tender* and 1 capful of *Sol-U-Mel* to a 16 oz spray bottle and fill with water.

NOTE: Always read and follow product packaging directions and warnings.

KITCHEN – CEILING & WALLS

Mix 1 oz of *MelaMagic* in a gallon bucket of hot water. Use a cloth to wash down the ceiling and walls with this solution. Let them air dry.

KITCHEN – COPPER

Pour 2 oz of *Tub & Tile* in a 16 oz spray bottle and fill with water. Spray this solution on any copper pieces. Wipe with a clean cloth.

KITCHEN – COUNTERS

For kitchen countertops add 1 tsp of *Tough & Tender* and 1 capful of *Sol-U-Mel* to a 16 oz spray bottle filled with water. Spray on the counters and use a clean damp sponge to clean. Alternatively try the *Tough & Tender Wipes* for a quick cleanup. For removing stubborn stains, use *Sol-U-Mel* full-strength. To disinfect use *Sol-U-Guard Botanical* as directed. **Never use *Sol-U-Guard* on natural stone surfaces.**

PreSpot works great on laminated countertops for tough stains. Spray it on and let it soak for a few minutes before wiping.

Never use *Tub & Tile* on marble or granite surfaces.

KITCHEN – FLOORS

Mix 1 oz of *MelaMagic* into a gallon bucket full of hot water. Mop the floor and let it air dry.

KITCHEN – OVEN

Mix 2 oz of *MelaMagic* and 1 capful of *Sol-U-Mel* in a 16 oz spray bottle and fill with water. Apply to the oven and let it set for 5 minutes. Wipe it with a damp cloth. If it is a major job, use a soft scrubbing pad and straight *MelaMagic*.

KITCHEN – SINK

For general cleaning, put a few drops of *Tough & Tender* or *Lemon Brite* in the sink and scrub with a soft brush or scrubbing pad.

Use full-strength *Tub & Tile* or *Diamond Brite* to clean the scuff marks off enamel sinks. Scrub the stains gently and then rinse. Repeat as necessary. You will be amazed!

You may also want to try the *Whitening Tooth Polish*. It is a wonderful enamel cleaner.

KITCHEN – STOVE

For minor stove cleanups, add 1 tsp of *Tough & Tender* and 1 capful of *Sol-U-Mel* to a 16 oz spray bottle filled with water. Apply and let it set for a few minutes before you wipe and dry the area.

For major clean ups, apply full-strength *MelaMagic* with a spray bottle or soft cloth. Let it set for a few minutes and then use a soft scrubbing pad to lift off the grime. Wipe with a damp cloth.

KITCHEN – VENTILATION HOOD

Clean all the ventilation hood surfaces with full-strength *MelaMagic*. Apply it with a damp sponge or cloth. Allow it to set for a few minutes and then wipe with a clean damp cloth or paper towel.

NOTE: Always read and follow product packaging directions and warnings.

LAUNDRY

Believe it or not, 1 pump (1 tablespoon) of **MelaPower 6x** is sufficient for an average wash load. If you have soft water or use a water softener, you may be able to use even less! For high efficiency washing machines, use **MelaPower 6x HE**. To brighten your load considerably, add 1 tablespoon of **MelaBrite 6x**. In all-white loads you may want to use 2 tablespoons of **MelaBrite 6x** for extra whitening.

MelaSoft can be added to the wash load or to the dryer, whichever is easier for you. For dryer use, just dampen a soft cloth with **MelaSoft** and throw it in the dryer with the wet clothes. Or use the convenient, ready-made **MelaSoft** dryer sheets.

If you are washing clothes that have mildew or any other type of odor, add 1 capful of **Sol-U-Mel** to your normal wash load. It is very effective. Some even recommend adding **Sol-U-Mel** to every load for the additional germ protection.

LAUNDRY – BLEACH SUBSTITUTE

Use **MelaBrite Color-Safe Whitener & Brightener**. You may want to use ¼ cup in a white load for extra whitening as opposed to just ⅛ cup in a regular load.

LAUNDRY – FINE WASHABLES

To launder wool, nylon, or other fine fabrics, add 1 tsp of **Tough & Tender** to a basin of cold water. Gently wash and rinse your fine washables.

LAUNDRY STAINS

Use **PreSpot**. It will take out almost all stains. Some stains will require full-strength **PreSpot**. However, many lighter stains will disappear with a 50% dilution just as well.

For challenging stains, allow the **PreSpot** to soak into the cloth before putting it in the washer. Sometimes it helps to scratch the stain or rub fabric on fabric. If the stain is still visible, repeat the process a time or two. Some find that it is even more effective if you moisten the garment first and then spray **PreSpot** on the moistened garment and let it set for a little while before washing.

If you temporarily run out of **PreSpot**, use full strength **Tough & Tender** on the fabric stain. After applying with a damp cloth, allow it to remain for a few minutes before rinsing.

If you have tried everything else and simply can't get a stain out of a white fabric, use Melaleuca's **Whitening Tooth Polish**. It is amazing on everything from polyester to cotton and even some delicate fabrics.

For removing red stains such as catsup, spaghetti sauce or blood, try rubbing the area with **Antibacterial Liquid Soap**. It works wonders!

If you are away from home, **Hot/Cool Shot Breath Spray** is the best as an instant spot and stain remover. Spray the spot with **Hot/Cool Shot** and then rub with a fingernail before rinsing with cold water. It's magic!

LEATHER CLEANER

Rustic Touch cleans vinyl and leather. It is also great for cleaning the dash of your car. **NOTE:** Spray it on a cloth to apply. If you spray it directly on the dash, you will get it on the inside of your windshield.

An alternate choice would be to use a 1:2 solution of **Antibacterial Liquid Soap** and water. It is very effective for removing dirt and scuff marks from leather.

NOTE: Always read and follow product packaging directions and warnings.

MAGIC MARKER

Concentrated *Sol-U-Mel* can be used to remove permanent marker stains, but you must be very careful that the surface to be cleaned has been sealed. *Sol-U-Mel* can remove a surface's finish.

MICROWAVE

Mix 1 tsp of *Tough & Tender* and 1 capful of *Sol-U-Mel* in a 16 oz bottle of water. Apply to the microwave and wipe it with a damp cloth. Alternatively, try the *Tough & Tender Wipes.*

MOLD & MILDEW See *Bathroom – Mold & Mildew*

ODORS

Use diluted *Sol-U-Mel* to eliminate odors of all kinds, including pet odors, smoke, and other strong odors. Spray in the air or on surfaces.

Sol-U-Guard Botanical has the great smell of thyme and will also kill germs that cause odors.

In the laundry, add 1 to 2 capfuls of full strength *Sol-U-Mel* to eliminate odors and boost the cleaning strength of *MelaPower*.

OVENS See *Kitchen – Oven*

PET ODORS See *Odors*

POTS AND PANS

Use *Tub & Tile* to clean stainless steel pots and pans, especially when they have been boiled dry or have baked-on grime on them. It seems to eat away at the black mess and make it much easier to restore to their original condition.

Tub & Tile is also very effective when cleaning copper pans.

REFRIGERATOR

Mix 1 tsp of *Tough & Tender* and 1 capful of *Sol-U-Mel* in a 16 oz bottle of water. Spray the inside and outside of the refrigerator with this solution and dry with a soft cloth.

For extra-strength disinfecting and deodorizing use *Sol-U-Guard Botanical*.

RUST

To remove rust stains from clothes, soak the area in concentrated *Tub & Tile*. When the rust spots have faded, wash as usual with *MelaPower* and *MelaBrite*.

Rust spots can be removed from a number of other surfaces by using *Tub & Tile* as well. **Just remember not to use it on marble or granite.**

SILVER CLEANER

Whitening Tooth Polish is excellent silver cleaner. Apply with a soft cloth and then rinse and dry. The shine will last much longer and is considerably safer than toxic silver polishes. (Save your empty tubes and when it is time to polish the silver, slice them open and you will find enough of the *Tooth Polish* residue to do quite a cleaning job. It is very economical, too!)

NOTE: Always read and follow product packaging directions and warnings.

TOYS

Frequently treat washable toys to a good soaking in a sink or container of water with 1 capful of *Sol-U-Mel* and 1 tsp of *Tough & Tender* added. After the toys have soaked, rinse them well and dry carefully.

Toys that cannot be soaked can be treated with *Sol-U-Guard Botanical* disinfectant as directed.

Machine washable stuffed animals, dolls, and blankets should be washed as usual with *MelaPower* (1 pump) and 1 capful of *Sol-U-Mel*.

WALLS

For a very effective general cleaning disinfectant, mix 1 tsp of *Tough & Tender* in a 16 oz bottle of water, or add 1 oz of *Tough & Tender* to a gallon bucket of water. If you need a stronger mixture, add 1 capful of *Sol-U-Mel* to either the spray or the bucket.

WINDOWS

Use *Clear Power* on the glass as directed. Clean with cheap paper towels. The Melaleuca products are effective enough to bring out the additives in the more expensive paper towels which can leave streaks. They can also release the ink on the newsprint from the old-time popular newspaper-cleaning trick. Old towels and cloths can leave lint. Cheap paper towels are by far the most effective when cleaning windows.

Also try using *Clear Power* diluted to ½ the strength recommended on the bottle. For most uses this is sufficient and even more economical.

WOOD FURNITURE

To clean dirt from wood furniture, mix 1 tsp of *Tough & Tender* and 1 gallon of water. Apply this solution with a rag or sponge. Carefully towel dry the furniture. For heavy stains, use 1 tbsp of *Sol-U-Mel* and 1 gallon of water. Finish cleaning with *Rustic Touch* and a soft rag.

WRINKLES – CLOTHING

When schedules have been too busy and you are just too tired to fold those freshly washed clothes, never fear, *Revive* is here! Just spray and shake the clothes and hang them or lay them over a chair until they dry. Not only will the wrinkles come out, but they will smell fresh, too. Some suggest diluting it by half. It seems to work just as well.

NOTE: Always read and follow product packaging directions and warnings.

SECTION FOUR

Healthy Dogs & Cats

PRECAUTIONS

If you are like most pet owners, your pets are very special to you. It is important to you to take the best care of them that you can. If you have not already done so, removing all of the grocery store brand cleaning and personal care products from your home is probably the easiest thing you can do to prolong the good health of your pets. Animals are more sensitive to toxic chemical vapors than we are because they are much lower to the ground where the vapors accumulate.

When using Melaleuca, or any other products, be sure to follow the package directions carefully. **When using *T36-C5* or *T40-C3* on your pets, apply a diluted solution to a small area and check for sensitivity for 48 hours.** If no reaction occurs, it should be safe. If at any time a reaction occurs, discontinue use immediately. Never use undiluted *T36-C5* on your cat. Never use *T36-C5* on a cat with impaired liver or kidney function, or on young kittens, without the guidance of a vet. See Recommended Dilutions below.

Always consult your veterinarian before starting any course of supplementation or treatment for your pet. Every effort has been made to ensure that the information contained in this book is complete and accurate. However, neither the publisher nor the author is engaged in rendering professional advice or services to the individual reader. The ideas, procedures and suggestions contained in this book are not intended as a substitute for consulting with your veterinarian. Neither the author nor the publisher shall be liable for any loss, injury, or damage allegedly arising from any information or suggestion in this book.

RECOMMENDED T36-C5 DILUTIONS

*Please Note: Use the lesser dilution on areas of sensitive skin. Any carrier oil can be used to dilute **T36-C5**, but it is worth noting that fractionated coconut oil is a light and fragrance-free oil that is very good for most applications. Jojoba oil is excellent for using on the coat and skin, if only a small amount is used it usually soaks in without leaving a greasy film. Olive oil is a much heavier oil, but has good anti-fungal properties.*

- ***Large Dog:*** Mix 3–4 drops of *T36-C5* in 1 teaspoon of carrier oil. Apply 2–3 times each day until healed.
- ***Medium to Small Dog:*** Mix 2–3 drops of *T36-C5* to every teaspoon of carrier oil and apply 2–3 times per day until healed.
- ***Puppies:*** Use the minimum dilution required that is known to be a broad spectrum antiseptic—2 drops of *T36-C5* to every tsp of carrier oil and apply 2–3 times per day. Do not use over a large area of skin.
- ***Adult Cats:*** Mix 2 drops of *T36-C5* in 1 teaspoon of carrier oil, mix well, and apply twice a day to the immediate area, until healed. Do not saturate the skin more than is necessary. If your cat is light haired or is a pedigree, there is an increased risk of an adverse reaction the stronger the dilution, the larger the area covered, and the longer it is used.

DOGS & CATS GENERAL INFORMATION

The fur and skin of most animals should not be overly washed with harsh detergents or shampoos. Cats and dogs can develop sensitivity and produce dry skin as a result of overwashing. Preventive care during seasonal infestation with fleas, ticks, mites and other insects can be accomplished by proper nutritional support to the animal. Dogs appear to have a particularly high requirement for extra calcium and magnesium. Cats appear to require additional B-complex, often in the form of brewers yeast. Dogs appear to fare very well when treated with *Sol-U-Mel*, *Renew Bath Oil*, and diluted *T36-C5*. Cats are more sensitive, and should not be treated with these products without consulting a veterinarian first. Optimum nutritional support should be provided based on the individual animal. Your natural veterinarian should be consulted if you are uncertain as to what your pet may need.

ABSCESSES

Dogs and cats often get into fights. It is a natural territorial trait. When the skin is punctured, infection can set in and an abscess is the most likely result. If the abscess is large, if it is situated in the mouth or near to an eye, shows no sign of improvement or the animal is in obvious distress, consult a vet as soon as possible. If the abscess appears to be hard or becomes hard, consult a vet. It may not be an abscess.

Dogs: At the first sign of a puncture wound or abscess, dab with a strong antiseptic mix of 5–10 drops *T36-C5* in a teaspoon of carrier oil.

Cats: At the first sign of a puncture wound or abscess, dab with a strong antiseptic mix of 5 drops *T36-C5* in a teaspoon of carrier oil.

Try to keep the animal from licking the area treated for at least 30 minutes after application. When the abscess bursts, allow it to drain and bathe the area with *Antiseptic Wash*, below. Keep applying the diluted *T36-C5* for 7 days.

ANTISEPTIC WASH

Dogs: Bathe wounds, bites, scratches, etc. with an antiseptic wash made by adding 2–3 drops of *T36-C5* mixed with 3 drops of carrier oil, added to a bowl of warm water.

Cats: Bathe wounds, bites, scratches, etc. with an antiseptic wash made by adding 2 drops of *T36-C5* mixed with 4 drops of carrier oil, to a bowl of warm water.

Agitate the water well to mix and apply to a localized area with a cotton ball. Bathe twice a day to help stop infection. For larger wounds, or wounds that are slow to heal, seek advice from a vet. After bathing, apply an antiseptic oil—either use a dilution of *T36-C5* that is appropriate for your pet or apply *MelaGel* to the area. See *Recommended T36-C5 Dilutions*.

ALLERGIES

Dogs: Just as in humans, allergies in dogs can be treated with *ProVex-Plus* and *Florify*. For larger breeds, give two capsules of *ProVex-Plus* and one capsule of *Florify* per day for the first month and then reduce to one capsule each per day. Give smaller breeds one capsule per day each and then reduce to one capsule each every other day after the first month. Open the capsules and mix it with

---

NOTE: Always consult your veterinarian before starting any course of supplementation or treatment for your pet. See *Precautions* and *Dilution Recommendations* for dogs & cats on page 55.

your dog's favorite food or the capsules can also be coated with malleable dog treats and offered to your dog. If the dog refuses to eat them, you can give the capsules whole. Hold the dog securely and open the mouth with your thumb and index finger each side of the dog's jaw, (with your palm underneath the lower jaw, about half way along). Apply gentle pressure and the mouth should naturally open. Move your thumb and finger further down to keep the jaw open. Tilt the head upwards and pop the capsules on the back of the tongue. Immediately hold the mouth shut, so that the dog cannot move the capsules with its tongue. Never apply more than gentle pressure and talk soothingly to your dog the whole time.

Cats: One *ProVex-Plus* capsule per day will help your cat deal with chronic allergies. Open the capsule and mix it with your cat's favorite food. If the cat refuses to eat it, you can give the capsule whole. Hold the cat securely; it may help to wrap it in a towel. Open the cat's mouth with your thumb and index finger each side of the cat's jaw (and your palm on top of the cat's head). Apply gentle pressure and the mouth should naturally open. Pop the capsule on the very back of the cat's tongue. Immediately hold the cat's mouth shut and up, so that it cannot move the capsule with its tongue. Never apply more than gentle pressure and talk soothingly to your cat the whole time. A *Florify* capsule, opened and mixed into drinks or food may also help allergies.

ARTHRITIS

Dogs: Painful inflammation of the joints usually causes a dog to limp. Some veterinarians are having excellent results using *ProVex-Plus* for arthritis in dogs. For larger breeds, give two capsules per day for the first month, then reduce to one capsule per day. Give smaller breeds one capsule per day and then reduce to one capsule every other day after the first month. Give the capsules to your dog wrapped in a piece of cheese or in the center of a piece of hotdog.

For immediate care, combine 1–2 drops of *T36-C5* with 1 teaspoon of Jojoba oil and very gently massage the arthritic area. If you follow with a heating pad, be sure that the setting is on low to prevent burning. A chopped up capsule of *Phytomega* can be regularly added to your dog's food, it can help to improve the suppleness of the joints. Dogs with arthritis can be given *ProCare Hip + Joint Treats for Dogs* powered by *Oligo* which is formulated with *Replenex* technology to help rebuild damaged and worn cartilage. *ProVex-Plus* helps to strengthen connective tissue and reduce inflammation. Both are good for reducing the severity of arthritis.

Cats: Combine 1–2 drops of *T36-C5* with 1 teaspoon of Jojoba oil and very gently massage the arthritic area. If you follow with a heating pad, be sure that the setting is on low to prevent burning. A chopped up capsule of *Phytomega* can be added to your cat's food, it can help to improve the suppleness of your cat's joints.

DERMATITIS

Skin conditions, such as rashes, flaky skin, redness, or itchiness, should be treated to prevent secondary infections and reduce any discomfort. You may need to keep the dog or cat isolated to prevent a contagious condition from spreading. Make sure that your pet has not come into contact with air fresheners, spray polishes, or other commercial cleaning products which may be a cause of

---

NOTE: Always consult your veterinarian before starting any course of supplementation or treatment for your pet. See *Precautions* and *Dilution Recommendations* for dogs & cats on page 55.

the problem. Switching to Melaleuca cleaning products will probably help your pet. Cut the hair around the affected area and wash with the *Antiseptic Wash* above. Pat the area dry. Apply **Renew Intensive Skin Therapy**, **Triple Antibiotic Ointment**, or a **T36-C5** Antiseptic Dilution 2–3 times for dogs (2 times for cats) each day until the condition improves. See your vet if the problem persists. See also *Mange*.

EARS

Dogs and cats often get ear infections. They can be caused by parasites or a scratch or bite from another animal. When treating the ears, use a dropper and massage the ears after medicating them. Be careful of the animal shaking its head. Do not put the dropper inside the ear. Apply a slightly warmed mixture of the following twice each day if possible until alleviated. Swab excess along the flap of the ear with cotton ball. Remember to always use a clean swab for each ear.

Dogs: Mix 1–2 drops of **T36-C5** with 2 teaspoons of olive oil, apply a couple of drops of this mixture to each ear as directed above. To discourage ear mites or to simply keep the ears clean, apply 1 or 2 drops of the above mixture on a cotton swab and wipe the inside of the ear every week.

Cats: Mix 1 drop of **T36-C5** with 2 teaspoons of olive oil. Apply a couple of drops of this mixture to each ear as directed above. To discourage ear mites or to simply keep the ears clean, apply 1 or 2 drops of the above mixture on a cotton swab and wipe the inside of the ear every 7–10 days.

FLEAS

If your pet is prone to pick up fleas, the best thing you can do is keep the fur well groomed and bathe with the following mixture:

Dogs: For every 2 teaspoons of **Melaleuca Original Shampoo** add 1 teaspoon Jojoba oil. Mix well. Shampoo the dog, avoiding the eyes and rinse well. Wash every week.

Cats: 1 teaspoon **Melaleuca Original Shampoo** and 1 teaspoon Jojoba oil. Mix and shampoo the cat avoiding the eyes. Rinse well. Bathe every 7–10 days.

Your pets should love the taste of Brewer's yeast, but fleas hate it. Why not give it a try, some pet owners swear by it.

HOT SPOTS – DOGS

Hot spots and abrasions on the body respond well to diluted **T36-C5** applied frequently to reduce the pain, prevent infection, and promote healing. **MelaGel** can be applied if drying or scaling results. **Triple Antibiotic Ointment** may help prevent the dog from chewing on the hot spots and making them worse. See *Recommended T36-C5 Dilutions* at the beginning of this section.

INSECT BITES & STINGS

Remove stinger. Apply diluted **T36-C5** (see *recommended T36-C5 Dilutions*) with a cotton swab to soothe the pain and neutralize the venom. If your pet is stung in the mouth by a bee or ant, apply bicarbonate of soda and ice and consult a vet as soon as possible. If your pet is stung in the mouth by a wasp, dab with vinegar and ice to avert swelling, and consult your vet as soon as possible.

NOTE: Always consult your veterinarian before starting any course of supplementation or treatment for your pet. See *Precautions* and *Dilution Recommendations* for dogs & cats on page 55.

LICE

Lice are species-specific. If a vet has determined your pet has lice, they are not the same head lice that often infest humans. Isolate your pet from other animals to keep the lice from spreading.

Dogs: Mix half to one teaspoon of *Sol-U-Mel* with 1–2 cups of warm water.

Cats: Mix half a teaspoon of *Sol-U-Mel* with 2 cups of warm water.

Place in a spray bottle and shake well to mix before each application. Spray the pet liberally with this mixture. Brush it in well to soften and dislodge the eggs of the lice. Let this stand for at least 10 minutes. Bathe thoroughly with *Melaleuca Original Shampoo* or *ProCare Pet Shampoo*. Pat dry with paper towels and dispose of the towels. Repeat daily until all signs of the lice are gone. Add 2 ounces of *Sol-U-Mel* to 16 ounces of water, and apply to areas where your pet sleeps or rests during the day and evening.

MANGE – DOGS

Mange is more common in dogs, and is generally caused by mites that bore into the skin and may be difficult to treat. If these suggestions don't work, contact your veterinarian. Isolate your pet to keep the condition from spreading to other animals.

Diluted *T36-C5* is very good for areas of unidentified rashes, it doesn't matter if it is Mange or any other cause, *T36-C5* is so broad-spectrum that it will help to alleviate itching and inflammation. Apply a mixture of 3–5 drops of *T36-C5* and 1 tsp. of Jojoba oil to the infected area twice a day.

For larger dogs and dogs that have no problem with Melaleuca oil, 10 drops per teaspoon of Jojoba oil may be applied. Dab it on with cotton ball. If no improvement within 4 weeks, or an adverse reaction occurs, discontinue use. See *Dermatitis*.

PAW ABRASIONS

Pets' paws can become cracked and sore. Bathe in antiseptic wash (See the *Recommended T36-C5 Dilutions* and *Antiseptic Wash*.) and apply a few drops of the following mixture:

Dogs: 5 drops of *T36-C5* blended with ½ cup of carrier oil. Store this mixture in a dark glass bottle and apply it to the paws 2–3 times each day.

Cats: 1–2 drops of *T36-C5* blended with ½ cup of carrier oil. Store this mixture in a dark glass bottle and apply it to the paws 2–3 times each day.

If your pet will wear little socks, it will assist in the healing and help to keep the area clean. An alternate solution is to treat paw abrasions with *MelaGel* or *Triple Antibiotic Ointment*. Apply twice daily as long as needed.

RASHES See *Dermatitis*

RINGWORM

Ringworm usually appears as a ring-shaped sore on the skin with patchy hair growth. It is caused by a fungus and is very contagious, so keep the pet isolated until the treatment is successful. Cut the remaining hair away from the affected area and wash thoroughly with the *Antiseptic Wash*.

Dogs: Apply a dilution of *T36-C5* (5 drops *T36-C5* in a teaspoon of olive oil) directly

---

NOTE: Always consult your veterinarian before starting any course of supplementation or treatment for your pet. See *Precautions* and *Dilution Recommendations* for dogs & cats on page 55.

to the area with a cotton ball 3–4 times a day. Be aware of any signs of sensitivity.

Cats: Apply a dilution of *T36-C5* (2 drops *T36-C5* in a teaspoon of olive oil) directly to the area with a cotton ball 2 or 3 times a day. Be aware of any signs of sensitivity.

Dermatin, *MelaGel*, or *Triple Antibiotic Ointment* are also effective. It may take a couple of weeks to clear up this condition. Make sure that your pet is well fed with the proper nutrition to help him fight the infection.

SKUNK ODORS – DOGS

When your dog has had an encounter in with a skunk, run a large outdoor tub full of water, add 3–4 tablespoons of sodium bicarbonate (bicarbonate of soda), and wash him/her with *Melaleuca Original Shampoo* or *Antibacterial Liquid Soap*. Let it stand for a few minutes then rinse. Repeat if necessary. (The next bath will probably need to be yours!).

NOTE: If a skunk has sprayed your pet, act immediately to eliminate the odor. The longer it stays on the pet, the more difficult it is to remove. Immediately rinse the pet with cool water. (Warm water only amplifies the odor.) Then wash and rinse as suggested above.

SPRAY – TOMCATS

Spraying is a natural habit for tomcats. They are marking their territory. Neutering the cat usually stops this annoying habit, but when a cat feels insecure by the addition of another pet, changing houses, etc., your tomcat could revert to his old ways again. Make your cat as secure as you can with lots of reassurance. Mask the area he sprays with a solution of 1 cup of hot water combined with a squirt of *Lemon Brite* and half a teaspoon of *Sol-U-Mel*. If all else fails and your tomcat is still spraying inside the home, fill a new spray bottle with water. When (and only when) you actually catch him spraying inside the house, give him 2–3 short bursts of water to his tail (always avoid spraying head and eyes). Within a few days he should get the message and stop spraying indoors. To clean those sprayed spots, pour diluted *Sol-U-Mel* onto the area and then spray with *Tough & Tender*. Wipe the area with a damp cloth.

SUNBURN – DOGS

Cool your pet down and give plenty of drinking water, apply *Renew Intensive Skin Therapy* or *MelaGel* to the area 2 to 3 times each day. Keep the pet out of the sun as much as possible. An alternate solution is to apply 2 drops of *T36-C5* in a teaspoon of vitamin E and jojoba oil to the sunburned area. Keep it cool and moist. Keep your pet out of the sun for at least a week.

NOTE: Always consult your veterinarian before starting any course of supplementation or treatment for your pet. See *Precautions* and *Dilution Recommendations* for dogs & cats on page 55.

Appendix

DISINFECTANT PROPERTIES OF T36-C5
COMPARED TO OTHER AGENTS

The following table is a summary of clinical research and is based upon direct contact of the agent with the organism. Standard concentrations were used. This demonstrates the disinfectant ability of Melaleuca alternifolia oil which contains at least 37% terpenols and less than 7% cineol. Please note that although many organisms show sensitivity to certain agents, mutant strains are developing which resist control. Many disinfectants are toxic or cause damage to skin when used over a prolonged time period. For these reasons, a number of these agents are no longer used clinically.

Disinfectant Agent	S	E	B	F	V	C	TOXIC?
Isopropyl Alcohol	K	K	O	P	P	O	
Phenolics	K	K	O	P	O	P	
Chlorine Solution	K	K	O	P	P	P	Yes
Iodine Tincture	K	K	O	P	O	P	
Acetaldehyde	K	K	P	K	K	K	Yes
Mercury Salts	K	P	K	K	K	K	Yes
Hexachorophen	K	P	O	K	O	O	
Quaternary Ammonium	K	P	O	P	O	O	
Boric Acid	P	P	O	O	O	O	
Cidex	K	K	P	K	K	K	
T36-C5	K	K	K	K	K	K	

K = Kills organism
P = Partially effective
O = Does not kill organism

S = Staph Aureus
E = E. Coli
B = Bacteria Spores
F = Fungi
V = Viruses
C = Candida Albicans

Technical Information

Although there are over 300 known species of tea trees *(Melaleuca)* in Australia, only one, the *Melaleuca alternifolia*, is known to have substantial therapeutic properties. The most closely related species to *Melaleuca alternifolia* is the *M. linarifilia* that yields an oil that is somewhat bacteriostatic, but is too high in Cineole, a natural skin irritant.

The pure oil of *Melaleuca alternifolia* is known to contain at least 100 compounds. A few of these compounds are not yet identified. A unique compound, viridiflorene, is found only to exist in oil of Melaleuca. Two other compounds, Terpinen-4-ol and Cineole, are regulated by the Australian Standards Association to designate therapeutic quality.

In Australia, the minimum amount of Terpinen-4-ol allowed is 30%, and the maximum amount of Cineole is 15%. Terpinen-4-ol is one of the more important therapeutic ingredients in the oil. Therefore, one would want oil high in Terpinen-4-ol. And since Cineole is caustic to the skin, the higher quality oil is low in Cineole. High quality oil should have at least 35% Terpinen-4-ol and less than 10% Cineole.

Since pure oil of *Melaleuca* is entirely natural and the genetics of one tree varies slightly from the other, the quality of oil from one grove of trees may vary substantially from another. In fact, much of the oil that has been distilled from *Melaleuca alternifolia* trees does not meet the minimum standards of quality oil.

Much research still needs to be done to determine exactly why *Melaleuca oil* works as it does and what extract proportion of each of the compounds produces the most effective blend of oil.

In order for any product to give repeatable, expected results, it must be consistent from batch to batch. For this reason, we strongly recommend that anyone purchasing products labeled as or containing oil of *Melaleuca* do so from a reputable firm that has its source of oil and quality of oil well documented.

The following lists 48 of the 100 known compounds in pure *Melaleuca alternifolia* oil.

48 of the 100 Known Compounds of Pure *Melaleuca alternifolia* Oil

1. α-Pinene
2. Camphene
3. β-Pinene
4. Sabinene
5. Myrcene
6. α-Phellandrene
7. 1,4-Cineole
8. α-Terpinene
9. Limonene
10. 1,8-Cineole
11. γ-Terpinene
12. p-Cymene
13. Terpinolene
14. Hexanol
15. Allyl hexanoate
16. α-p-Dimethyl-styrene
17. β-Phellandrene
18. α-Cubebene
19. (a Sesquiterpene)
20. α-Copaene
21. Camphor
22. α-Gurjunene
23. Linalool
24. (a Sesquiterpene)
25. α-Thujene
26. 1-Terpineol
27. 1-Terpinen-4-ol
28. β-Elemene
29. β-Caryophyllene
30. (a Sesquiterpene)
31. Aromadendrene
32. β-Terpineol
33. Allo-aromadendrene
34. Globulol
35. α-Humulene
36. *tr*-p-menthen-2-ol
37. γ-Muurolene
38. α-Terpineol
39. Viridiflorene
40. Piperitone
41. α-Muurolene
42. Piperitol
43. Viridiflorol
44. δ-Cadinene
45. 4,10-Dimethyl-7-isopropyl bicyclo [4.4.0]-1,4-decadiene
46. Nerol
47. 8-p-Cymenol
48. Clamenene

Product Price Comparison

WalMart vs. Melaleuca

Survey Date: Oct 26, 2011 (WalMart in Centennial, Colorado)

WALMART	Size/Use	No. of Uses Per Purchase	Ratio* to Melaleuca	Cost of Each Pkg.	TOTAL COST
Tide Liquid	150 oz.	96 loads	1.00	$ 17.97	$ 17.97
Bounce Dryer Sheets	80 sheets	80 uses	1.25	4.24	5.30
Windex Glass Cleaner	32 oz.		3.00	2.47	7.41
Tilex Bathroom Cleaner	32 oz.		3.00	3.98	11.94
Windex Wipes	28 wipes	28 uses	1.07	2.87	3.07
409 Degreaser	32 oz		3.00	1.98	5.94
Listerine Total Care	33.8 oz.		.95	5.78	5.49
Glide Dental Tape	54.7 yds.		1.01	3.37	3.40
L'Oréal Sulfate-Free Shampoo	8.5 oz.		1.41	5.97	8.42
Lamisil Antifungal Ointment	.42 oz.		1.19	8.84	10.52
Tylenol PM	100 caplets	100 uses	.50	10.72	5.36
	SUB TOTAL				$ 84.82
	Tax (6.85%)				5.81
	WALMART TOTAL				**$ 90.63**

MELALEUCA	Size/Use		No. of Uses Per Purchase	Ratio* to Melaleuca	PC Cost of Each Pkg.	Total COST
MelaPower 6x Laundry	48 oz.	=	96 loads	1	$ 16.99	$ 16.99
MelaSoft Dryer Sheets	100 sh.	=	100 uses	1	5.69	5.69
Clear Power Glass Cleaner	16 oz.	=	96 oz.	1	5.69	5.69
Tub & Tile Bathroom Cleaner	16 oz.	=	96 oz.	1	5.69	5.69
Tough & Tender Wipes	30 wipes	=	30 uses	1	3.49	3.49
Tough & Tender Cleaner	16 oz.	=	96 oz.	1	5.69	5.69
Breath-Away Mouth Rinse	8 oz.	=	32 oz.	1	5.69	5.69
Classic Dental Floss	55 yds.			1	3.99	3.99
Affinia Sulfate-Free Shampoo	12 oz.			1	4.99	4.99
Dermatin Antifungal Creme	.5 oz.			1	7.89	7.89
CounterAct PM	50 caplets		50 uses	1	4.09	4.09
	SUB TOTAL					$ 69.89
	Shipping ($3.90 + 5.4% of order total)					7.67
	Tax (6.85%)					4.79
	Less Loyalty Shopping Dollars					−4.00
	MELALEUCA TOTAL					**$ 78.35**

WALMART TOTAL	=	$90.63
MELALEUCA TOTAL	=	$78.35
MELALEUCA SAVINGS		***=$12.28***

* For example: it takes three 32 oz. bottles of Tilex to equal one bottle of *Tub & Tile*.

Book Ordering Information

Melaleuca Quick Reference

(prices are in US dollars)

Quantity	Price Each
1–9	4.95
10–24	3.95
25–49	3.50
50–99	3.00
100–249	2.50
250+	1.95

The Melaleuca Wellness Guide

(prices are in US dollars)

Quantity	Price Each
1–4	12.50
5–9	10.75
10–19	9.50
20–49	8.25
50–99	6.95
100+	5.75

IF ORDERING BY PHONE (US and Canada)

We accept all major credit cards and ship most orders the same day we receive them. Smaller orders are shipped by First-Class Mail or Priority Mail. Larger orders are shipped by United Parcel Service. Call:

Toll-Free 1 (888) 209-0510

Local (303) 326-0626
Fax   (303) 568-0224

IF ORDERING BY MAIL (US and Canada)

Call us first to obtain your order total. We accept money orders (payable in US funds) or US checks. We usually dispatch mail orders the day after we receive them. Smaller orders are shipped by First-Class Mail or Priority Mail. Larger orders are shipped by United Parcel Service. Send order to:

RM Barry Publications
P.O. Box 3528
Littleton, CO 80161-3528

OTHER COUNTRIES (Australia, New Zealand, etc.)

Place orders online at: **www.rmbarry.com**

Questions? Email us at: **info@rmbarry.com**